E. B. Segel

English
National
Opera
Guide

2

Aida Verdi

D0452235

Giuseppe Verdi 1813 — 1901

Preface

English National Opera Guides are intended to be companions to opera in performance. They contain articles and illustrations relevant to any production and not only those mounted by English National Opera. Of general interest, also, is the inclusion of the complete original libretto of the opera, side by side with an English translation. There are many reasons why sung words may not be clearly distinguishable, whatever the language and however excellent the performance. The composer may have set several lines of text together, for instance, or he may have demanded an orchestral sound through which no voice can clearly articulate. ENO Guides supply English readers with an opportunity to know a libretto in advance and so greatly increase their understanding and enjoyment of performances whether live, broadcast or recorded.

We hope the Guides prove useful to new and experienced opera-lovers alike. An audience which knows what to look and listen for — one that demands a high standard of performance and recognises it when it is achieved — is our best support and, of course, an assurance for the future of opera in the English-speaking world.

Nicholas John
Editor

AIDA

Giuseppe Verdi

English National Opera Guides Series Editor:
Nicholas John

John Calder ● London
Riverrun Press ● New York

First published in Great Britain, 1980, by
John Calder (Publishers) Ltd., 18 Brewer Street,
London W1R 4AS
and
in the U.S.A., 1980, by
Riverrun Press Inc.,
175 Fifth Avenue,
New York, NY 10010

© English National Opera 1980

Verdi's 'Egyptian business'
© Michael Rose 1980

'*Aida:* Text and Music'
© William Mann 1980

'The Genesis of Aida'
© Roger Parker 1980

Extracts from the translations by Hans Busch reproduced by courtesy of the
University of Minnesota Press © 1979

English Version © Edmund Tracey 1980

ALL RIGHTS RESERVED

ISBN 0 7145 3770 5   Paperback edition

BRITISH LIBRARY CATALOGUING DATA

Ghislanzoni, Antonio
    Aida. — (English National Opera guides; 2).
    1. Operas — Librettos
    I. Title   II. John, Nicholas   III. Tracey, Edmund
    IV. Verdi, Giuseppe   V. Series
    782.1'2   ML50.V484

No part of this publication may be reproduced, stored in a retrieval system,
or transmitted, by any form or by any means, electronic, mechanical,
photo-copying or otherwise, except brief extracts for the purpose of review,
without the prior written permission of the copyright owner and publisher.

Any paperback edition of this book whether published simultaneously with,
or subsequent to, the hardback edition is sold subject to the condition that it
shall not, by way of trade, be lent, resold, hired out, or otherwise disposed
of, without the publisher's consent, in any form of binding other than that
in which it is published.

Typeset in Plantin by Alan Sutton Publishing Limited, Gloucester
Printed by Whitstable Litho Ltd in Great Britain.

Contents

List of Illustrations

Verdi's 'Egyptian Business'

Michael Rose

"If anyone had said to me two years ago 'You are going to write an opera for Cairo', I'd have said he was mad — but now I see it's me who is mad. . . ."

You can look at *Aida* as an Egyptian opera, a French opera or an Italian opera. For most people, perhaps, it is the Egyptian aspect that predominates. *Aida* is the Grand Opera of all Grand Operas, *the* great operatic spectacular: tunes, choruses, trumpets; vast crowds, monumental sets; armies, temples, Egyptian priests, Ethiopian slaves, horses, camels, elephants — the lot. And all written, incredibly, to open the Suez Canal. . . .

The interior of the Cairo Opera House showing the box on the left reserved for the Khedive's harem. Although the première (and indeed the dress rehearsal) of 'Aida' were received with the greatest enthusiasm by a packed house, which included the Khedive, the audience comprised chiefly Europeans. A fez was a rare sight in the opera house.

That, at least, is the legend. And it is true that, ever since the celebrations which surrounded the opening of the Canal in 1869, the Khedive of Egypt had been anxious to secure Verdi's co-operation in writing a work especially for Cairo. But the draft of a letter written by Verdi's wife in August of that year makes it clear that the original request was for a 'hymn' and not for an opera, and that the occasion was to be the inauguration of the Cairo Opera House, built to celebrate the opening of the Suez Canal, rather than the opening of the Canal itself. In any case, Verdi refused and the Opera House opened with *Rigoletto* on November 1, 1869. It was not till nearly three weeks later that a French ship, bearing the Empress Eugénie, steamed into Suez at the head of a cortège of sixty-eight vessels of various nationalities, and the Canal was formally opened to traffic.

Nevertheless, the Khedive's hopes of getting an opera out of his favourite composer were by no means dashed, though to begin with he met with no more luck than any of the other friends, acquaintances and interested parties who, ever since *Don Carlos*, had been plying Verdi with suggestions for a new libretto. Chief among these was Camille du Locle, the Director of the Paris Opéra-Comique, who now acted as intermediary in the Egyptian negotiations: to him wrote Mariette Bey, the great French Egyptologist and founder of the Cairo Museum, expressing the disappointment of the Khedive who was 'greatly vexed at the idea of giving up the collaboration of M. Verdi, whose talents he holds in immense esteem', and adding: 'A last word. If M. Verdi still does not accept, His Highness requests you to try knocking at another door. . . . There are ideas of Gounod, even Wagner. If the latter would do it he might produce something *grandiose*'. It is tempting to wonder whether the last phrase of this letter, which Du Locle astutely sent on to Verdi, may have had something to do with the composer's change of heart. But Du Locle enclosed at the same time a scenario of the proposed opera actually written by Mariette Bey (though at this stage, rather naively, Verdi was encouraged to believe that the Khedive himself had had a hand in it) — and in the end what undoubtedly drew Verdi's interest was, as always, the quality of the story itself.

The Egyptian aspect of the opera is one that has loomed very large in the development of the *Aida* legend, and indeed the popular idea of ancient Egypt is to a great extent encapsulated for us in this most successful of all Verdi's works. Clearly the archeological framework of the subject was one of the things which first tickled Verdi's imagination: it was something new, something different, which he felt would get him out of the rut of the usual operatic settings, and from the beginning he was much concerned about the historical details of the scenario. He pestered his publisher, Giulio Ricordi, with demands for information — was ancient Egyptian worship reserved exclusively for men? was Ethiopia the same as Abyssinia? which of the Rameses might correspond to the King in the opera? where and how were the mysteries of Isis celebrated? He extracted from a friend who had lived in Egypt three closely written pages about the ancient Egyptian

Costume design by Mariette Bey (courtesy of the Bibliothèque de l'Opéra, Paris) for an Ethiopian prisoner

religion, its beliefs, prayers, music and dances, and through Du Locle kept closely in touch with Mariette Bey, to whose original scenic ideas he clung through all the changes in the text as being far more authentic than anything he or Ghislanzoni could think up. Mariette was helpful about the music too. The sacred dance, he wrote, was probably accompanied by a kind of chant, forming the bass to a very high chant above it which was executed by young sopranos: the instruments accompanying it would have been harps with twenty-four strings, double flutes, trumpets, drums, large castanets and cymbals. Verdi actually went to Florence to examine an Egyptian flute in the museum there — but was disappointed to find that it was 'just a reed with holes in it, like our shepherds have'. And the details of staging and costumes were supervised by Mariette with scrupulous care: he was even worried about the personal appearance of the Italian singers, and wrote to the Director of the Cairo Opera, 'I really must speak to you seriously about this question of the actors and their moustaches and beards. . . . I know from experience that in Italy they don't trouble to get everything exactly right, and in *Aida* it is absolutely essential that there are no beards or moustaches. . . . I consider this a matter of life and death for the opera. . . .'

It is in the first two acts, with their religious and triumphal ceremonials, that the historical details are most in evidence, reaching a climax in the visual and musical splendours of the Triumph Scene, the biggest and best of many such scenes in nineteenth-century French and Italian opera. For Mariette, with his romantic vision of the grandeur of the Kingdom of the Pharaohs, this was an essential scene, in which all the elements of ancient Egyptian greatness could be paraded in a monumental setting with glittering ceremonial and a vast panoply of musical effect. For Verdi, however, once he had worked himself into his subject, the archeological trappings began to assume less importance, and became simply a background against which he was able to concentrate on the human situations which were the real stuff of the drama. (As he said in another context: 'To copy reality can be a good thing, but to invent reality is better, much better'.) Nevertheless, he had recognised from the beginning that this was a work which, if it was to live up to the spirit of its commission, must be 'of vast proportions, as if it were for that great barn of an opera house in Paris', and there is no doubt that the whole musical and scenic conception of *Aida* owed a lot to the traditions of Parisian Grand Opera.

Paris, with its sophisticated, cosmopolitan attitude to music and the theatre, was the recognised operatic centre of Europe, the magnet which attracted all the major nineteenth-century opera composers at some time or other, not always with the happiest results. Verdi had twice attempted a work there on the grandiose scale demanded by French operatic taste, but *Les Vêpres siciliennes*, in 1855, was dogged by libretto trouble, production difficulties and recurring threats of cancellation, and even *Don Carlos*, for all its great qualities, had somehow missed a real success. Verdi had therefore already decided that he would not again write an opera for the 'Grande Boutique'. But however unsatisfactory his personal experience in Paris may have been, he was far too good a composer not to have gained some positive advantage from the French connection, and what in fact emerged in *Aida* was a Grand Opera with some of the attributes of its Parisian model but without the complexities and conventions that were the bugbear of the Parisian style.

To a great extent this was due to the simplicity of the plot. The story of *Aida* is far more direct and single-minded than the complicated series of episodes and characters which make up the libretto of *Don Carlos* — indeed, it has often been criticized for going too far in the opposite direction. But the change was deliberate, and the result a quicker, clearer and more continuous articulation of the drama, and a more immediate identification with the characters and their feelings. At first glance it may seem that this is confined to the more intimate, personal episodes of the opera: the first scene of Act Two, the Nile Scene, or the final duet. But this is not really the case. The same consistency of dramatic intention lies behind the big spectaculars, into which the dramatic conflict is woven with unfailing care and consistency. Take the Triumph Scene again: as spectacle it is magnificent, and perfectly adapted both to the occasion for which it was written and to its position in the opera. It is the kind of thing that Meyerbeer did, only not quite so well. But its very success in these respects has tended to obscure not only its extraordinary melodic vitality and cumulative musical invention (Meyerbeer, in all his glory, never came near to this), but also its place in the drama. And the crucial dramatic point on which the triumph scene turns is the entry of Amonasro, father of Aida and King of the defeated Ethiopian people.

Amonasro is patriotism incarnate, and it is only with his appearance on the scene that we realise that patriotism is really what *Aida* is about. All his life, Verdi had been a passionate supporter of the cause of Italian nationalism: the success of *Nabucco* and the overwhelming popular reaction to the chorus '*Va pensiero*' were only the first indications of a vein of patriotic sentiment which burst out again and again in his earlier operas and made him, as his fame increased, into one of the figureheads of the *Risorgimento*. By the time *Aida* was written the situation had naturally moved with the years: Verdi was a national figure, a great admirer of Cavour, and after the unification of Italy under Victor Emanuel II of Piedmont in 1861 he had been persuaded, much against his will, to act as a deputy in the first Italian parliament. But the role never suited him, and his political views remained always instinctive and human, rather than in any way professional. And so in *Aida*, where the conflict is between Radamès's love for Aida and love for his country on the one hand, and Aida's similar emotional struggle on the other, the question is: whose side was Verdi really on?

From one point of view it is easy enough to see the tremendous parade of ancient Egyptian nationalism which runs through the earlier scenes of the opera as a very thinly disguised celebration of the spirit of the new Italy. The setting and subject of the Triumph Scene may be Egyptian, its theatrical conception Parisian, but its musical content remains obstinately Italian and the Grand March, for all those gorgeous 'Egyptian' trumpets which Verdi invented specially for the occasion, would be (and frequently has been) perfectly at home in the piazzas of Rome, Milan or Turin. The nobility of the King and the repressive conservatism of the High Priest are absolutely in line with such a view — indeed the sanctimonious attitude of the priesthood is a specially Verdian touch. He wrote to Ghislanzoni about a point in the libretto for this scene: 'You must alter the first eight lines of the chorus and add eight more for the priests to the effect that "we have conquered with the help of divine providence. The enemy is delivered into our hands. God is henceforward on our side". (See King William's telegram).' The reference is, of course, to the famous message sent by the King of Prussia to his queen after the victory of Sedan, news of which reached Italy as the Triumph Scene was being written. Although it didn't work out quite as blatantly as that in the final libretto, it is amusing to see the words of the German King being attibuted to the priests rather than to the titular head of ancient Egypt. To Italians of Verdi's generation France had always been considered the natural ally of Italy, and when the Franco-Prussian war broke out in 1870 Verdi's sympathies were with the French: in spite of his distrust of Napoleon III he saw a powerful German Empire, united under the iron control of Bismarck, as just as serious a threat to Europe and Italy as ever Austria had been, and it is characteristic that he should have identified this aspect of European politics with the group that, in his own country, he had always seen as the main opponent of Italian progress.

Nevertheless, whatever the implications of Egyptian nationalism as an allegory of the contemporary situation in Italy, there is no doubt that the true drama of *Aida* originates in quite another quarter. To this drama the display of Egyptian power and state-consciousness is an essential adjunct, because it gives concrete, visual expression to one side of Radamès's predicament. But the entry of Amonasro makes it perfectly clear where Verdi's sympathies lie: whatever the musical seductions of Pharaonic grandeur, the emotional impetus of the opera comes from Ethiopia, and its ultimate protagonist is not Radamès, or Amneris, or Ramfis, or the King, but Aida herself. In the end, Verdi was nearly always on the side of the underdog: '*Va pensiero*' is the song of the underdog in exile, and the patriotic nostalgia of the Jews during the Babylonian captivity is not much different in kind from the patriotic nostalgia of Aida and Amonasro in Egyptian servitude. In the days of *Nabucco*, Italy was herself the underdog: by the time of *Aida*, however, the new Italian state no longer saw itself like that and Verdi, who was proud of his country and its achievement, was prepared to celebrate the new spirit. Yet — Bismarck, Napoleon III, wars and aggression and displays of strength — these were manifestations of a national obsessiveness that were a far cry from the human patriotism of the *Risorgimento*, and so there is in *Aida* a confusion of patriotic feeling, a double tug at the national heart strings, which reflects something very real in Verdi's state of mind and provides at the same time the background, and even to some extent the motivation, for Radamès's tragic dilemma.

Now in all this there is, in the end, very little that is Egyptian and not much that is French. Yet there is a lot that is Italian, and not only from a political point of view. All through the opera, and in the last scenes particularly, there is a concentration on the essence of the drama, and an insistence on the direct dramatic impact of the singing line, that is profoundly Italian. Verdi refines yet again on the continuity of musical texture which he has been developing ever since *Rigoletto*, through *Simon Boccanegra*, *Un Ballo in Maschera*, *La Forza del Destino* and even *Don Carlos*, but here the simplicity of the story allows him to bring together all his mature experience, the Parisian part not forgotten, in a parallel simplicity of human dramatic treatment. His letters to Ghislanzoni are filled with warnings to write directly, naturally, without the clichés of the typical opera libretto, with an overall result that is poles apart from the elaborate theatricality of the Parisian manner and the novelty-seeking ingenuities of Meyerbeerian Grand Opera.

In a letter to Du Locle, written after the production of *Don Carlos*, Verdi had expressed his feelings as an Italian composer in Paris: 'In your musical theatre there are too many connoisseurs! Everybody wants to judge for himself, according to his own tastes and, what is worse, according to a *system*, without taking account of the character and individuality of the composer. Everyone wants to give an opinion, express a doubt, and a composer, living for long in this atmosphere of uncertainty, can hardly help being shaken in his convictions and ends by correcting and adjusting, which really means spoiling his work. In this way the final product is never an opera created in a single jet, but a *mosaic* — as beautiful as you like, but still a *mosaic*. . . .'

13

It is because *Aida*, for all its monumental framework and archeological paraphernalia, is fundamentally an opera 'created in a single jet' that it has outlived, and will continue to outlive, so many of its Grand Operatic fellows. For all the refinement of method and richness of musical idiom, it is an opera in the same tradition as *Nabucco* or *Trovatore*, transformed by a master into something which takes it even beyond a narrow national idiom and into a world of its own. 'I believe in inspiration, you believe in construction', he wrote in the same letter; 'I want the enthusiasm that you lack, both in feeling and judgement. . . . For me, true success is not possible unless I write as I feel, free from any outside influence whatever, without thinking whether I write for Paris or for the moon. . . .'

Aida a lunar opera? That would perhaps be going too far. But to let it get stuck at the Egyptian level is certainly not going far enough.

Eva Turner as Aida, Chicago Civic Opera, 1928 (by courtesy of the Covent Garden Archives)

'Aida': Text and Music

William Mann

Ever since its Cairo première in December 1871, followed a month later by the Italian première at La Scala, Milan (for which Verdi composed an Overture which was not played, though it survives), *Aida*⋆ has been acclaimed as a non-pareil spectacular opera, an almost automatic choice for a grand operatic occasion, the epitome of Grand Opera in the French tradition of the Rossini of *Moïse* or *Guillaume Tell* and Spontini. Very splendid it looks in the monumental open-air productions at the Caracalla Baths in Rome or the Arena of Verona; Mariette Bey (he had been ennobled by the Khedive) noted initially that the first scene would show a distant view of the Pyramids at Memphis, and Ghislanzoni's final stage directions specify unusual stage effects in every scene. Both scenes of the last act, for example, involve action, although not necessarily visible, on two levels.

Verdi's score, nevertheless, concentrates on a private drama between three principal characters, Radamès and the two women who love him. The fourth principal character is the Egyptian priesthood, whose spokesman is the High Priest, Ramfis, rather than the Ethiopian King, Amonasro, whose demands precipitate the tragic dénouement but whose role is otherwise almost subsidiary to the plot. Verdi used certain characteristic themes (similar to Wagner's *Leitmotiven* except that they are hardly developed symphonically) principally in order to draw attention to a particular identity or emotion — Aida [1] and the Priests [2] have one each, Amneris has two [4, 5]. They are sparingly reintroduced, each time to cogent purpose. By the time that Verdi came to compose *Aida* he had, like most of his operatic contemporaries, abandoned separate musical numbers and was writing virtually uninterrupted scenes to maintain dramatic continuity, though he did, in some cases (for example, after '*Celeste Aida*', but not after '*O patria mia*'), end a set piece with a tactful pause during which the audience could express appreciation, or otherwise, of the singing.

The musical structure of *Aida* is both refined and diversified in proportions, pace, and mood, above all in texture, whether orchestral, vocal, or both together. Because the score is melodically profuse, and contains those spectacular mass ensembles, some past commentators, when only a few operas by Verdi were well known, used to regard *Aida* as the end of the 'middle period' which began with *Rigoletto*, and was succeeded by the succinct 'late period' of

---

⋆ In Italian the first two letters of her name ('ai') are always pronounced separately, as in 'naïve' not as the dipthong in English 'plaice', German 'Hain', or French 'Laine'.

Otello and *Falstaff*. Now that all of Verdi's music can be heard, thanks to radio, records, and a much expanded stage repertory, we are likely to reject the 'three periods' view of Verdi, and set *Aida* where it belongs, in the continuous chain of Verdi's musical development, every work looking forwards and backwards at once.

The old-fashioned operatic overture, which began and ended noisily, was necessary in theatres where the auditorium lights were never extinguished, late-comers an occupational hazard, and the composer's duty was to alert the attention of every listener. The *Preludio* to *Aida* begins softly with muted strings by themselves, violins divided two and two; the third act will also begin softly, a reminder that by 1871 it was physically possible and aesthetically desirable to extinguish the house lights before the music began, so that the audience would, with any luck, be silent and able to attend to 'soft music and sweet harmony'.

Aida begins with the theme [1] for that lady held as a prisoner of war and ranked as a slave, though her Egyptian captors are unaware that she is the daughter of the Ethiopian King. She is, for the moment, kindly treated by the Egyptian princess Amneris to whose handmaidens she has been assigned. Her theme is wayward and desolate, regal pride subsumed by her unpromising fate: Ethiopians and Egyptians have long been at war (it is perhaps about 1000 BC, the time of the Trojan War), Egypt numerically superior, Ethiopia plucky and persistent. The key of the Prelude is D major, but more melancholy D minor is quickly suggested, and the theme comes to rest in F sharp major, the key in which the opera will end. This appealing tune grows and expands, with soft added flute and clarinet, rousing emotions of pity and love for Aida. Still very softly, muted cellos introduce the stubborn theme of the Egyptian priests, [2], taken up in contrapuntal imitation by higher strings, then woodwind. Almost at once Aida's theme is combined with it, loudly: it is the dramatic confrontation of the opera, Ethiopia against Egypt, one powerless, lovable woman against another nation's might. The full orchestra is involved. The confrontation fades away, leaving divided first violins with Aida's melody, cadenced, cushioned by wind, rising aloft.

The curtain rises on Pharaoh's palace in Memphis. Radamès, the captain of the Pharaoh's Guard, and the high priest Ramfis are conversing about the new invasion of Egypt by Ethiopian troops. The key has changed to G major, one step away on the flat side, conveying relaxation (key progressions in tonal music, whether flat or sharp, always have a clear emotional effect). Ramfis's opening remarks are sagely accompanied by imitative priestly counterpoint for three groups of cellos, sometimes joined discreetly by violas, all dark in tone. Ramfis leaves to tell Pharaoh the name of the chosen general, and Radamès, an ambitious dreamer, wishes that he might be the divinely selected leader. Brassy fanfares echo his wish and bring maximum contrast to the preceding soft music. When he thinks of Aida, in whose name he would fight and conquer (though against her own kinsmen!), gentler strings support his utterance and when he launches into his first aria, after a further fanfare, two muted violins gently breathe a high sustained F to inspire his amorous reverie.

'Celeste Aida' [3] is placed close to the beginning of the opera as if to make an immediate declaration of intent by Verdi: Aida will abound in long melody and bel canto, gratifying and challenging the greatest Italianate voices of every generation to sing with as much subtlety and discretion as the orchestra which accompanies them. Twice in his Romanza Radamès rises to a forte top B flat but he begins and ends softly (though few modern tenors respect the pianissimo morendo, presumably indicating head-voice, attached to his last high B flat). His melody is delicately, elegantly phrased, doubled at first by low flute, actually a sixth above him, though effectively a third below, since the tenor voice gives the illusion of sounding an octave above its real pitch (except in concerted vocal ensemble). The scoring of this solo is a miracle of delicacy: lower strings are plucked, with a buoyant rhythmical pattern for cellos; violins are among them, except for six soloists who shimmer aloft (Verdi, marked them a parte, ' separately disposed'). After the fourth line, before 'Il tuo bel cielo', both flutes begin to undulate, still in their low register, below oboe and bassoon in tenths who introduce the singer's new melody for those words. At 'un regal serto' the pace slightly quickens, and the texture is enriched towards the first climax at 'un trono vicino al sol' whence the music returns to the opening, 'Celeste Aida', newly and more elaborately accompanied until 'sei lo splendor'. Here a variant of the oboe-bassoon tenths persists while Radamès repeats 'Il tuo bel cielo' to a soft low monotone, breaking out into melody at 'un regal serto', and returning quickly to pppp after his second high B flat. The ending, darkly luminous, should sound wondrously tender with hidden depths of sincerity beneath his gentle ardour.

As the solo ends (without the conventional quicker second section, now repudiated by Verdi 'unless there is dramatic motivation for it'), the Egyptian princess Amneris enters, introduced by her theme of smooth, stately graciousness (first violins on their lowest string) [4]. She remarks teasingly on his eager expression of joy, following but not doubling her theme, and is unconvinced by his talk of military aspiration. Does he not cherish dreams of love ('Ne un altro sogno mai')? — and violins slide into a wheedling phrase, concerned with her secret passion. Typical of the late Verdi's methods are the oboe's openly quizzical acciaccature at 'Non hai tu in Menfi', and the clarinet's echoes of the music for those words. This moment of intensity marks the approach to a Duettino, *Allegro agitato presto* in E minor (*'Forse l'arcano amore'*), which will eventually become a Terzetto after Aida's entrance. The duet begins the second of Amneris's recurrent themes, subdued and anxious, representing Radamès's guilty secret as much as Amneris's desperate jealousy [5]; it is another long, expanding melody. As it peters out, Aida enters *Andante mosso* to her theme [1], frail and pensive on clarinet. Amneris scents a possible rival and the Duettino is resumed with its scurrying tune. Amneris controls her jealousy and, *Andante* in C major, turns graciously to Aida, with another stately tune, calling her sister rather than slave. Flute and oboe — *acciaccature* again — show that Aida is in tears, as Amneris observes in a cadencing phrase which looks forward to Desdemona pleading for Cassio in the second act of *Otello*. Aida blames the fearful rumours of war, *più mosso* with grand expansion at *'per voi pavento'*. In a deadly hush Amneris asks if that is the whole truth. Aida casts down her gaze to hide her real anxiety, and the Duettino is resumed for the third time, becoming a Trio in E major, around the suspicion *motiv* [5], as Aida's voice is joined with the alternate mutterings of the others in a broad melody which confesses aside her tearful, hopeless love for Radamès; softly, in the background, timpani depict the uneasy pounding of their three hearts.

The trio ends with a hectic return to E minor, and a diplomatic pause for audience participation, before trumpets and other brass dispel those three conflicting and private disquiets with loud fanfares of public pomp, dark and savage — the noisy string trills anticipate Verdi's music for Iago (in *Otello*). Pharaoh, with his captains, ministers, and priests led by Ramfis, arrives to proclaim the renewal of war against Ethiopia, calling on a Messenger to disclose his news (a doleful E minor phrase for oboe, clarinet and bassoon, then loud explosive leaps for the amazement of the listening crowd). The Messenger announces that the invaders are led by an indomitable warrior, Amonasro: the crowd knows him as the Ethiopian king but, we now discover from her aside, he is also Aida's father. 'Battle' is the inexorable cry (*'Guerra'* — full chorus and orchestra). In recitative, Pharaoh announces the goddess Isis's choice of Radamès to lead the Egyptian army — joy for him and Amneris, despair for Aida, surprise for the rest. He is sent by Pharaoh to be armed and consecrated in the temple of Ptah (the king uses the god's classical Italian name of Vulcano), and a pompous march-ensemble is launched (*'Sù! del cor prorompa il grido'*) [6] with much xenophobic declaration of *'morte allo stranier'* (lit. 'Death to foreigners')! It ends with Amneris's call to Radamès, repeated by all, of *'Ritorna vincitor'!* Then Aida is left alone, asking herself how she could bear to wish anyone victory over her own father, family and compatriots.

This is her extremely famous and beloved *Scena e Romanza* [7], known by the opening words of its introductory recitative, those with which Amneris and the Memphides have just sent Radamès off to war, namely, '*Ritorna vincitor!*' (whereas most operatic solos are called by the first words of the subsequent aria). As a musical entity it has begun, not with Aida's first words, nor with the march reprise preceding them (usually used as prelude when the solo is performed by itself), but with Amneris's cry before that, an example of Verdi's drastic break with the conventional 'number-opera'. The traditional form of the solo aria was in two sections, slow and quicker, but '*Ritorna vincitor*' is in five sections. First comes a recitative, *Allegro agitato*, with orchestral comments about Egypt's might and the doleful fate foreseen by Aida for her family. Then, after a pause, a faster passage, '*L'insana parola*', urgently melodious with prominent bassoon backing, comes to an alarmed climax ('*Ah! sventurata!*'). The third section brings back Aida's *motiv* [1] from the Prelude, *Andante* ('slower than the first time', said Verdi), and edges between aria and recitative; it is followed by a fast, agitated, melodious section, '*I sacri nomi*' [8] in A flat minor full of triplet movement and easing into the *cantabile* final section, '*Numi, pietà*' [9], infinitely touching with its tremulous string background. '*Numi, pietà*' will be heard again, though it is not a true *Leitmotiv*.

It ends with cellos descending to their bottom C, thence climbing the arpeggio of A flat major to pause on its fifth, E flat, whose major mode begins the next scene. The music continues without a break for the scene change. It would be a thrilling surprise to hear the E flat major harp chords break into the cellos' last note, if only because operagoers have learned to accept a wait while the set changes. The temple of Ptah in Memphis is another grand setting with columns stretching back out of sight, and statues, and tripods exuding incense around the central altar of the divinity. The High Priestess (identified as Termouthis by Mariette Bey), invisible to us, is invoking '*Possente Fthà, del mondo spirito animator*' to a designedly exotic melody, almost in the Phrygian mode [10]. She is answered by Priests gathered on stage. Three times the hymn is heard, with off-stage priestesses to join Termouthis. Then comes a Sacred Dance of Priestesses [11], somewhat faster, in E flat major, featuring three flutes (a hallmark of this score), elements of the Phrygian mode, and those biting *acciaccature* which Verdi must have have likewise thought Egyptian-sounding. The dance must be extremely solemn and rather mysterious to accord with its music: this is, after all, a sacred rite. Halfway through it, the strings move purposefully and Radamès, unarmed, is brought to the altar to be invested. The Dance ends with a brief choral antiphony of priestesses and priests.

The Temple of Ptah in the 1979 ENO production designed by Stefanos Lazaridis

Ramfis, in a new section of recitative, consecrates Radamès
(*'Mortal, diletto ai numi'*) as leader of the Egyptian army, investing
him with the sacred sword; heavy brass and chorus confirm the
solemnity of the ceremony. Strings softly slide into solemn G minor
for a broad-phrased prayer to Ptah (*'Nume, custode e vindice'*) [12]
in which he is joined gravely by Radamès and the priests, and
which acquires brilliance as well as weight as its melody is combined with the Priestesses' hymn. Just before the close of the scene,
and act, there is a sublime, unaccompanied cry of *'Immenso Fthà!'*

Act Two takes place in Thebes, some 400 miles upstream from
Memphis, and begins in Amneris's apartments where she is being
ceremoniously attired for the triumphal return of Radamès from
the wars. Loud strumming in G minor upon the harp, distantly
punctuated by a solo trumpet, suggests the martial occasion. A
chorus of female slaves hymns the victorious hero (*'Chi mai fra
gl'inni'*) [13] who will be rewarded (refrain of rising scales at *'Vieni:
sul crin ti piovano'*) with floral tributes. Amneris adds her own love-
call in G major, rather chromatic and totally haunting, marked 'ex-
pansively' so that the most can be made of these amorous phrases
(*'Ah! vieni, amor mio'*) [14]. A second, similar verse follows, then a
jolly G minor Dance of Moorish slave-boys, [15] with triangle and
cymbals and piccolo (relics of 18th century Turkish music!); lastly

a third repeat of the double refrain from Amneris's handmaidens and herself (*'Vieni: sul crin'*, etc.).

Aida's theme [1] (now in the bass) indicates her approach. The other slaves are dismissed so that their mistress may unfathom Aida's secret (a telling unaccompanied signal on solo horn indicates her intention with characteristic brevity — throughout *Aida* Verdi unconventionally marks dramatic turning-points without making a meal of them). *Moderato* in A major, Amneris solicitously begins her great Scena and Duet with Aida by feigning consolation for the other's grief in the defeat of her compatriots, and protesting her love for her slave. Aida's hectic protestations (bassoons and lower strings hint at Amonasro to come) do not disturb Amneris's condescending sweetness: Aida must find consolation in love. She touches a raw spot, as throbbing string bass triplets and woodwind counterpoint, surrounding Aida's animated asides (*'Amore! gaudio, tormento'*) [1], leave no doubt. In the same triplets Amneris welcomes her breakthrough (*'Ah, quel pallore'*) and proceeds to her subterfuge.

To a new, slower melody [16] that by now seems familiar because so characteristic of Verdi's music for Amneris, extravagantly gracious, almost toadying, on oboes, clarinets and first violins in B flat major, she asks (*'Ebben: qual nuovo fremito'*) for Aida's confidence as to whether she has a lover in the Egyptian army. Her carefully restrained quizzing is reflected by gentle clarinets in consoling thirds and sixths over bassoons, which somehow suggest raised eyebrows. After all, she hints, the army's leader has been slain. There are sounds of agitation on strings as Aida learns Amneris's false report of Radamès's death. Aida is plunged into grief. Amneris suspects the worst and confirms it by then declaring that Radamès still lives — news which brings Aida to her knees in gratitude, and lifts her to an exultant top A calling, for a moment, on the full orchestra's force. A sinister, brusque slither for bassoons and lower strings gazes deep into Amneris's scheming soul, and shows the fatal blunder of Aida's outburst. Like a cat who has cornered a mouse, Amneris gloats: 'with maximum fury' writes Verdi over her words *'Si . . . tu l'ami'* ('you love him? I love him too . . . you understand? You see your rival . . . I who am Pharaoh's daughter'), but he partners them sarcastically with soft clarinets in smiling thirds, and the bassoon and horn who underpin *'son tua rivale'* sound anything but enraged.

Aida's heart beats wildly, and she retorts, with passion until she reaches *'tal'* (implying that she and Amneris are 'alike' of royal blood), when the orchestra holds its peace, and we appreciate her timely embarrassment. Her confusion brings back full orchestra, again for only an instant, as she realizes how nearly she implicated the rest of her family, as well as herself, perhaps all Ethiopia, in this private quarrel. Her only recourse can be apologetic self-abasement, which we hear in abject F minor, *Adagio cantabile* [17], her supple melodic line coloured by low flutes (later clarinets, for more warmth) and put in focus by the bassoon's harmonic outlines — how often, in this opera, Verdi shows us the physical aspect of his characters, as well as their emotions. Amneris knows that she has won this match, and she could afford, after this handsome apology, to react with kindness but she needs to savour her triumph, even over a slave. She explodes with scorn (*'trema, vil schiava'*) [18] and unbecoming brusqueness. Aida resumes her self-abasement, this time as a duet.

Amneris's private triumph is mirrored publicly by the offstage military band's fanfares, and the distant choral salutation in A flat major [6] to Radamès on his victorious return from the wars. We might have assumed that the duet was over, and that the off-stage chorus and band were preparing for the scene-change, but they have motivated a quicker closing section. Aida bewails her misery in A flat minor and willingness to placate her rival by dying. Amneris's reply in fulsome A flat major is that of a domineering schoolmistress dragging her errant pupil off to be seen by the Head, but it reaches a massive climax, dispelled as Amneris leaves. Before the curtain falls, Verdi makes Aida repeat her prayer *de profundis* from the end of *'Ritorna vincitor.'* It was a melodic moment worthy of reprise, and justified by the turn of events: then Aida feared for her lover and her country, now her compatriots are vanquished, her lover apparently lost to her not through death but through power politics. This time *'Numi, pietà'* [9] has no closing cello solo but an even more forlorn fade-away on shuddering strings with plucked bass.

Verdi seems to have intended a pause until the curtain is ready to rise again for the *Gran Finale secondo* with the military band in position on stage. Producers can keep the music running, by using a narrow stage for the first scene, and removing its furniture during the fanfares and dark-toned expectant music on the verge of E flat major, gradually brightening with the trumpet entry, so that the brightly lit stage, filled with people, is seen when that key arrives. The score does show that Pharaoh, Amneris with Aida and others enter just before that, and dramatically it is best if the curtain can rise as soon as possible. The choral outburst of *'Gloria all'Egitto'* [19] with stage band and full orchestra is like a sudden flood of brilliant sunlight, tempting to the producer seeking a dramatic *coup.* Experiencing it at the first performance, the Khedive wished it might be adopted as the Egyptian National Anthem — or did he mean the March trio section [20] in A flat with massed trumpets (which is more melodious)? The E flat part of this March is quite subtle for public purposes, with essential dynamic contrast and shading, including a very refined, almost fragile turn into the second subject for female chorus, followed by the Priests [2], and then both choruses in fervent unison. Now comes the most famous tune of all, the Trio section [20], specifically for Egyptian trumpets — the long ones, which used to be called Bach trumpets, pitched in A flat and subsequently in B natural. The melody deserves its fame, being muscular and vivacious in gait, its fanfare character enhanced by the insistence of the prolonged first cadence, declaring as it were, 'This is the conqueror, yes he's the one, it's him, he's the one we're saluting'. The trumpets are crooked in two keys because, when the tune has been played, it is at once repeated in another key, and then, most effectively, both groups play together.

A Ballabile, that is a dance, follows in C minor [21], rather faster, during which the captured treasures of the Ethiopians are displayed. Its music is also of great subtlety: staccato flute triplets over a chugging bass, with a melodious countersubject for bassoon and violas, the whole sounding gaunt and official, yet animated. The chirpy grace-notes, in the F minor trio-section, [22] excuse the usual gollywog disguise of the dancers, though the text does not specify a return of the Moorish boys. The dance is gleeful and exotic, perhaps even a little conspiratorial. Afterwards comes a choral reprise [19] of the salute to Radamès, again involving the Priestly theme, then a coda with the female chorus, extended to include everybody.

Pharaoh descends from his throne to welcome Radamès: the stage band responds enthusiastically. Amneris is called to lay on his head the victor's laurel wreath, a signal for her solemn, regal theme, heard in the first scene [4], sumptuously set for violins on their rich G string, with undulating clarinet arpeggios, and pale flutes: we 'hear' pallor and grandeur at once, because Amneris knows that Radamès loves another. Now Pharaoh offers to fulfil Radamès's greatest wish. He ought to ask for the hand of Aida but he presumably thinks the moment is inappropriate, since he asks instead that the Ethiopian prisoners be brought in. They are led on while the Priests chant a variant of their *motiv*, which is singularly gloomy for a hymn of thanksgiving to the gods. Among them is Amonasro, dressed as an army officer. Aida's cry of recognition is echoed with surprise by everyone else: 'Her father!' Quietly he tells her not to betray him; bassoons, cimbasso (preferred by Verdi to the modern tuba), and lower strings thunder out a *motiv* of majestic size whose rhythm and shape persist into his solo *'Anch' io pugnai'*. Familiarly known as the *'Sortita d'Amonasro'* or 'Entrance of Amonasro', this is a marvellous piece of character-portrayal through music with its dark, sturdy colours and grand melodic line at *'Al mio piè'* (Amonasro pretends that he saw the Ethiopian king dead on the battlefield). It culminates in the serene cantilena of

'*Ma tu, Re, tu signore possente*' [23], which is repeated by Aida and the other Ethiopians, with delicate wind accompaniment. Contrast comes with the vigorous objections of Ramfis and the other priests to any thought of mercy for these prisoners [24]; and from here Verdi builds up a grand ensemble, with a softer contrapuntal centre and a cadenza-like flourish for Aida before the reprise of '*Ma tu, Re*', and an energetic coda. There is a pause for admiration after the final cadence (and amid all the eloquence, we may still have missed Radamès's amorous asides as he watches Aida, and Amneris's rage as she observes him).

Radamès, as his favour, asks Pharaoh to release the Ethiopians and send them home ('What? All of them?', is Amneris's typical comment). Ramfis counsels against such unwisdom and finally persuades Pharaoh at least to keep Aida and her father in Egypt as hostages. The King then gives Radamès the hand of Amneris in marriage, and the promise of eventual succession — which draws another gloating aside from the bride-to-be, to a phrase which may come to mind during her ordeal in Act Four. Band and Chorus resume their hymn [19], '*Gloria all' Egitto*', with a separate vocal part for Pharaoh. The Priests add a new melody, Aida and Radamès a third one, all in enthusiastic style (though the new material is marked down to pianissimo) and in E flat major. Much faster, and in the minor, Amonasro whispers to Aida that they will soon be revenged on Egypt, and the soloists all indulge private reflexions in counterpoint while the choruses prepare for a return to the Triumphal Hymn now combined with its two succeeding tunes. A faster reprise of the Priests' *motiv* [2] leads to a grand coda incorporating the massed trumpets' March Trio tune [20].

Act Three is subtitled *The Banks of the Nile*. Camille du Locle's scenario specifies palmtrees growing amongst granite rocks upon the summit of which stands the temple of Isis, half-hidden by leafy branches. It is a starry, brightly moonlit night. Verdi's orchestral introduction depicts all this with flute solo and strings, a miracle of atmospheric loveliness, and of restraint: four octaves of staccato G, *molto pianissimo*, on muted first violins, then sustained Gs for cellos in glassy harmonics, three octaves of slower staccato Gs on muted violas, and a shimmering tremolo for muted second violins on G and D, yielding a mere sensation of open fifths in G upon which the flute dips and sways exotically. From the temple the priests and their priestesses are heard invoking the mother-bride of Osiris. As they chant, a boat glides down the river, bringing Amneris and Ramfis, with guards and veiled handmaidens, to the temple. Gentle strings accompany Ramfis as he invites the princess to pray in the temple until dawn for the blessing of Isis on her marriage to Radamès next day. Her agreement brings a new mood for Amneris, simple and girlish, slightly hesitant and with a magically benign cadence. As they enter the temple the introductory music is resumed, now combined with the chorus and two priestesses. As it dwindles to two solo violins on high G, three flutes bring back Aida's *motiv* [1], violas murmuring below. Aida enters cautiously, wondering why Radamès has asked her to meet him here; if it is to say farewell, she will drown herself in the Nile (a short but vivid orchestral tempest). That would mean that she would never again see her native land, as she reflects in the Romanza, '*O patria mia*', which Verdi added at the last minute with Theresa Stolz, the first Aida at La Scala, in mind. It is difficult to imagine the opera, let alone the third act, without it. The oboe solo's introductory bars pursue the curiously exotic vein which was Verdi's vision of African music (I have drawn attention to other examples). Aida's first two lines are in arioso style but the Romanza begins, melodically, at the third line, '*O cieli azzurri*' [25], with prominent flute trio again, and a memorable reshaping of her first phrase ('*O patria mia*') at '*O verdi colli*'. Throughout the Romanza, Verdi's F major has tendencies towards D minor which contributes to the exotic effect and, at the end of the first verse (there are two), her top A is unexpectedly but affectingly harmonised as a first inversion A minor chord, another modal effect. Her second verse adds to the three flutes some active solo strings to enhance the chamber-musical intimacy. The verse now ascends to a soft top C, and ends with an exquisite (and testing) long, phrase beginning on her top A, climbing down to middle C, then back again with oboe and flute as Aida's partners. We can find precedents for the musical refinement of this Romanza in *Simon Boccanegra* and *Don Carlos*, for instance, and still it seems unmatched in Verdi's work.

A solo clarinet muses gently on the '*O patria mia*' theme, then breaks off. Aida sees her father approaching. The shock is reflected by loud strings in E flat major, an abrupt drop of a whole tone. Amonasro's first sentences of recitative seem to look back thematically to his *Sortita*, perhaps only inasmuch as Verdi was composing consistently in character. At '*E patria, e trono*', Amonasro eases with dignity into melodiousness, in preparation for the first of the two duets, side by side, which carry the weight of the act after the Romanza. This first duet, '*Rivedrai le foreste imbalsamate*' [26], is formally tripartite: a wooing, cantabile *Allegro giusto* in D flat major, with a tougher episode at '*Pur rammenti*', and a return to lyricism at Aida's '*Ah! ben rammento*' (a glance at the libretto will explain this), after which the section turns towards recitative, until Amonasro reveals Aida's task. When she refuses, the second, more dramatic section begins, Allegro in C minor, '*Su, dunque! sorgete, egizie coorti*' [27] (almost unnecessarily marked 'with savage impetus', so mordant are the brilliant trumpet parts). Amonasro's music of conspiracy ('*Flutti di sangue scorrono*'), scare-mongering

('*Una larva orribile*'), and open threat ('*Non sei mia figlia*') look forward to Verdi's Iago but are recognizably in the character of the warrior who sang the *Sortita*. Soft cello arpeggios again suggest Aida's abject distress. It is the bassoon, with low strings, which sets the tone for the final section of the duet, *Andante assai sostenuto* in D flat, '*Padre a costoro schiava non sono*', expanding from near recitative into noble melody at Amonasro's '*Pensa che un popolo*' [28], during which the violins rise steadily and momentously through Aida's reply to an apex at '*Quanto mi costi*'. Then darkness descends again and Amonasro leaves Aida alone to deceive the man she adores.

Radamès hurries to meet Aida. Anxious exchanges for violins and cellos suggest the lovers hailing one another. The second of the two duets begins with a swaggering, confident tune for Radamès's '*Pur ti riveggo*' [29], all careless C major extraversion, like himself. Each of his joyous exclamations is doused by Aida's assumed coolness and scorn, while the melody continues darkly in the orchestra. Radamès stands up for his optimism ('*Nel fiero anelito*') with another martial theme for trumpet duet, which is distinctly likable; in his confidence he returns to complete his enthusiastic opening tune. Aida reminds him of jealous Amneris, and Verdi reverts to

Nellie Melba as Aida
(Philadelphia, 1898)

the scurrying theme [5] of the duet (*'Forse l'arcano amore'*) upon which she intruded in the first scene. He uses this technique of thematic back-reference quite seldom but always with particular cogency — once in most of the mature operas, and several times in *Aida*. She assures Radamès that his optimism is hopeless, and proposes that their only future together lies in escape to Ethiopia. His shocked astonishment allows her to launch a new section, a wheedling pastoral which opens with an oboe solo (more exotic chromaticism), and truly begins at *'Là, tra foreste vergine'* [30], again blessed with three prominent flutes (once too often, one might fear, but the charm still works). Radamès's answer is more frankly melodious in character (*'Il suol dov' io raccolsi'*) while the willowy pleading of her melody is now resumed as a simultaneous duet which repeats both melodic halves. In semi-recitative Aida goads Radamès until he agrees to run away with her: the third section of the duet, *'Sì: fuggiam da queste mura'* [31], now begins, impetuously but for the most part softly, with a generous yet rather stiff tune, sung by both, and leading to a reprise in unison of the duet's intitial melody [29].

It breaks off as Aida turns to ask, in recitative, where the Egyptian army is posted. Amonasro leaves his hiding-place to repeat the words triumphantly. Radamès is appalled that he has been overheard and to discover Amonasro's real identity. The resultant Trio begins in semi-recitative, turning to memorable melody at Aida's *'Ah no! ti calma'* (consoling in D flat minor) answered in proud despairing D flat major by Radamès, and benignly by Amonasro, a rich complex of three splendid tunes, worthy of ample development were it not that the drama must press forward. Before the Trio can expatiate, Amneris appears outside the temple and precipitates the dénouement, not with an aria, or even a vocal quartet, but with the one word *'Traditor!'*. Amonasro, prevented from stabbing her, escapes with Aida in a coda of confusion and high drama, broken for Radamès's characteristically heroic gesture of self-sacrifice, before the final rush of D minor. The third act of *Aida* stands up to the closest scrutiny. It is the finest scene in the opera, and for some ardent Verdians excels anything even in *Otello* and *Falstaff* to come — though among such exalted company it is idle to pick favourites.

Act Four has two scenes. The first shows a hall in Pharaoh's palace connecting the cell, where Radamès is imprisoned, with the subterranean vault where he is to be tried. Woodwind stride softly down the arpeggio of G minor, notably the eerie voice of the piccolo. We may imagine Amneris swooping down some large staircase to this hall, where she paces anxiously to and fro as her nervous jealousy theme [5] (from the first act duet) suggests — it is soon deployed in contrapuntal imitation by strings, and is accompanied by undulating flutes, with soft yet distinct cries on piccolo (those *acciaccature* which have featured earlier in the score). Her movements may be deduced from the music; the stage directions merely place her 'sadly crouched in front of the door of the vault'. She is enraged that her rival has escaped while her bridegroom is incarcerated on a charge of treason. She was his accuser, yet she still loves him — a return to her stately theme from the Triumph Scene. She decides to save him, even now. Verdi lets us hear her ponder how to do it, then sense her decision, as she orders the guards to bring him to her.

The music for his entrance is woeful with cor anglais prominent, then bass clarinet whose drooping arpeggios launch their big duet, *'Già i sacerdoti adunansi'* [32]. It is marked *Andante sostenuto* in the dark key of E flat minor, and is relieved, as though by a shaft of sunlight, when the last two lines of the verse move into the relative major and a warmer orchestral texture. It is at such moments of transition from one mood to another and back that a composer reveals mastery: the move to G flat major enables Radamès to repeat the music in the second verse, and in a key (F sharp minor, enharmonic with G flat) better suited to his vocal compass, ordinary clarinet replacing bass clarinet. After some tense exchanges in A major, the key reached at the end of Radamès's verse, Verdi screws the music up another third to D flat major for Amneris's next entreaty, *'Ah! tu dêi vivere!'* [33], a confession of love and longing, and therefore a melody of brighter, aspiring cast. Radamès repeats its last phrases with reference to his love for Aida. Mention of her rival inflames Amneris, and Radamès quickly returns to the key and melody of *'Già i sacerdoti'* [32], rounding off this section of the duet. The approach to the subsequent, faster part is made via agitation: Radamès rejects Amneris's offers, confirms his devotion to Aida, and resolves to pay the extreme penalty. Amneris bursts out in tearful C minor, *Allegro agitato vivo*, *'Chi ti salva, sciagurato'*, doing her best to harden her heart, the music declares, against him. Radamès answers calmly in C major (though the orchestral background remains agitated) but they end their interview to her C minor tune, and an inconclusive coda as he returns to his cell. The orchestral postlude gives a shattering glimpse of her utter despair (whether by accident or design, it repeats the rising-third key-switches from the start of the duet).

Crashing full chords, with pauses in between, draw attention not only to her loneliness and misery but to realization of the fatal consequences of her jealousy. Promptly enter the orchestral double basses with the Priests' theme, [2], its periods pointed by three soft trombones, until it becomes the gloomy march to which they process across the stage and down to the vault, while Amneris mutters helplessly her guilt in delivering him into their jurisdiction

('*Io stessa lo gettai*' — her woebegone reiterations stamp the phrase on the memory). From below, the Priests are heard in unaccompanied unison. Amneris answers it with her own distraught A minor prayer. They resume their chant as Radamès is led below. Amneris is left whimpering alone.

The trial begins in the vault. Three times Ramfis, assisted by four trumpets, four trombones, and bass drum, all sounding from the judgement chamber, calls on Radamès to answer the charges. Each time he remains silent, and Amneris hysterically entreats the gods to save him: the musical effect is as if the spotlight on her during her exclamations were extinguished whenever the drama moves to the vault below (visible in some productions). After Amneris's third plea, Ramfis and all the Priests announce their verdict in loud, strongly rhythmical unison with full orchestral punctuation: to be buried alive beneath the altar of Ptah. Amneris rails against the unyielding judges as they return [2], inveighing against the traitor. She pleads with them once, reviles them in an ensemble, and finally curses them. The scene ends with a raging orchestral coda that includes a stern unison figure which will be heard again. The last note of the coda involves the crash of a tamtam (a rimless gong with a fine resonance).

Verdi particularly requested that the final scene should take place on two levels, the upper stage showing the brightly lit and gorgeous interior of the temple of Ptah, the lower part the vault in which Radamès is left to die. During the introductory bars, two priests are supervising the closure of the stone at the top of the steps by which the victim has entered his execution-chamber. This is the temple in which Radamès was consecrated during the second scene of Act One. The kinship of the loud string phrases at the end of the preceding scene, and the wan echoes which begin this last scene, will be clear if the scene-change has been rapid. Radamès muses on his dismal fate. Then, as he thinks happily of Aida, a faint radiance falls from the string harmonies. Flute and oboe sigh a falling octave on Aida's behalf, for she has hidden here to be with Radamès at the last. The impassioned descending string chords (first inversions) after her opening words perfectly convey Radamès's amazement. Her explanation ('*Presago il core*') is sepulchrally scored for low clarinet, bassoon, bass drum and low strings with plucked double-basses, a timbre looking forward to the last act of *Otello*.

Her decision to die with him seems to banish Radamès's gloom, for his response in A flat major, '*Morir! si pura e bella!*' [34], is not only tender but buoyant with its plucked strings, comments for flute and oboes, and cosy chains of clarinet thirds. This is the introduction to the final Duet, arguably the most magical in the opera's rich series of duets. Aida's reply, [35], in delirious D flat major ecstasy, has an elaborate and luminous accompaniment, first violins divided into four groups, as if one were watching a starry galaxy through a telescope. Their euphoria is interrupted by the prayers of priests and priestesses in the temple above (with a harp on stage) [10]. Radamès, bravely but in vain, attempts to lift the seal-stone. Flutes recall part of the Priestesses' Dance, from Act One, scene two, as the lovers resign themselves to fate.

Aida begins the final duet proper, '*O terra, addio*' [36], with another, paler, luminous string texture, a melody in G flat major that hauntingly rises an octave via the seventh degree, again and again. When Radamès repeats the melody, with comments from her, the luminous strings are a little more animated. Again the Priests in the temple invoke Ptah (in a different part of their hymn). Amneris enters the temple and kneels in prayer upon the 'fatal stone', as Radamès and Aida in unison approach the third and last verse of their duet, this time with a simpler shimmering orchestral background, and with intervening orisons from Amneris. The lovers add a last, crowning line to their melody, then embrace as Aida dies. A solo violin recalls their melody above the chanted prayers in the temple. *Aida* ends quietly, as it began. To investigate its score, even as cursorily as here, is to marvel at the profusion of delicate, restrained, highly subtle effects, including soft, elegantly nuanced singing. They far outnumber the grand, full-throated climaxes which probably brought us to *Aida* in the first place. Verdi had been commissioned to supply a stirring nationalistic spectacle, and he obliged where necessary, but he expended his genius on what is most touching and durable in Mariette Bey's story, the secret places of human hearts.

The Genesis of 'Aida'
Roger Parker

It is well known that the pace of Verdi's creative output slowed considerably as he became older. The steady stream of new operas which had appeared in the 1840's and 1850's gradually dwindled, and the composer's violent, energetic imagination seemed to lose its confident voice. There are many explanations for this decline in productivity. One is undoubtedly that Verdi's inherent pessimism, fuelled by the deaths of many of his friends and by chaotic developments in the international political situation, led him to distrust the usefulness of composing as a way of life. Another is his increasingly firm financial position: earlier in his career, during the so-called 'galley years', his activity seemed fired by a frenetic desire to achieve financial independence. There is also evidence to suggest that he was undergoing an artistic crisis. Possible operatic subjects were picked over endlessly, only to be rejected for vague reasons of 'coldness' or 'lack of power' — the comparison with Puccini's unproductive maturity is unmistakable—; there is not the same dynamic enthusiasm which characterised his earlier years. This apparent diffidence had much to do with the direction in which Verdi saw his career moving. The triumphant successes of the early 1850's (*Rigoletto*, *Il trovatore* and *La traviata*) gain much of their effect from a strong unity of conception, while the operas which follow are painted on a broader canvas, with a greater variety of style and effect. This gradual change certainly brought Verdi nearer to the French grand opera tradition, but advance in one direction caused problems in another: the unity which characterised the finest early works was lost. Verdi expressed this in a letter to Camille du Locle, his co-librettist for *Don Carlos*, the opera written immediately before *Aida* (Paris Opéra, March 1867). Du Locle's attempts to interest the composer in further French projects stimulated a lengthy reply, which has been partly quoted on page 13. Although on the surface it is an attack levelled at the *mores* of the Paris Opéra, it seems in context to contain an implicit self-criticism by Verdi of his more recent works:

> [. . .] *Hélas*, it is neither the labour of writing an opera nor the judgement of the Parisian public that holds me back but rather the certainty of not being able to have my music performed in Paris the way I want it. It is quite singular that an author must always see his ideas frustrated and his conceptions distorted! . . . You will argue that the *Opéra* has produced a string of masterpieces in this manner. You may call them masterpieces all you want, but permit me to say that they would be much more perfect if the *patchwork* and the adjustments were not felt

all the time. Certainly no one will deny genius to Rossini. Nevertheless, in spite of all his genius, in *Guillaume Tell* one detects this fatal atmosphere of the *Opéra*; and several times, although less frequently than with other authors, one feels that there is too much here, too little there, and that the musical flow is not as free and secure as in the *Barbiere*.[. . .] (December 8, 1869)

It is against the background of this statement of policy, this passionate concern with the unity of a dramatic statement, that the music of *Aida* gradually evolved.

In spite of the apparent rebuff, du Locle continued to discuss possible, operatic subjects with Verdi. Finally, in May 1870, a breakthrough occurred. Du Locle sent the outline of an Egyptian plot for approval. It was greeted with genuine, if guarded, enthusiasm:

[. . .] I have read the Egyptian outline. It is well done; it offers a splendid *mise-en-scène*, and there are two or three situations which, if not very new, are certainly very beautiful. But who did it? There is a very expert hand in it, one accustomed to writing and one who knows the theatre very well. Now let's hear the financial conditions from Egypt, and then we shall decide. Who would have the Italian libretto made? Of course it would be necessary that I myself have it made. [. . .] (May 26, 1870)

As soon as Verdi showed an interest, matters moved very quickly. The composer's demanding terms, which included a fee of 150,000 lire, were immediately accepted on condition that the opera be ready for the following January. Verdi's enormous fee seems to have caused him a little embarrassment. As he wrote to du Locle:

We must at least keep the fee secret, since it would serve as a pretext to disturb so many poor dead men. Someone would be sure to point out the *400 scudi* for the *Barbiere di Siviglia*, *Beethoven's* poverty, *Schubert's* misery, *Mozart's* roaming about just to make a living, etc., etc. [. . .] (June 18, 1870)

For his librettist, Verdi chose Antonio Ghislanzoni, who had already helped with the revisions to *La forza del destino*, performed at La Scala in February 1869. The composer and his wife first made an Italian translation of Mariette's French outline and then, between June 19 and 26, Verdi and du Locle prepared a scenario which shaped the already detailed situations into dialogue form. Except in a few minor cases, the scenario keeps very close to the outline, again demonstrating Verdi's faith in Mariette's theatrical sense. A brief quotation from Mariette's first scene will demonstrate the detail he included, and how much of it was incorporated into the final text:

[. . .] Amneris is assailed by cruel doubts at Rhadames's coldness. A rival is certainly contending for Rhadames's heart. Who is it? Aïda, the Ethiopian slave who fell into the hands of the Egyptians after a recent victory, appears at the rear of the stage. An ardent look from Rhadames, a long sigh from Aïda threaten to reveal everything. Some instinct tells the princess that her rival is the slave she sees before her. At the moment when they, to themselves, are expressing their love, their lamentations, their displeasures, their sorrows, an officer of the king's household announces that his majesty is coming to the hall to receive a messenger sent by the governor of the Egyptian provinces bordering on Ethiopia. [. . .]

After Verdi and Ghislanzoni had met in mid-July, the librettist was sent away with du Locle's scenario to begin work. As a draft libretto gradually arrived by post, Verdi replied to Ghislanzoni with an almost line by line commentary, frequently requesting revisions, cuts and additions. Between August 12, 1870 and January 13, 1871, there survive no less than thirty-four letters from composer to librettist, constituting one of the most detailed documentary sources we have for the genesis of a Verdi (or indeed, any) opera. Before examining some of the major themes presented in this invaluable correspondence, a note of warning should be sounded. If read out of context, the letters may give the impression that once Verdi had established the text of a passage, his process of composition was virtually complete.

This impression is strengthened by the extreme speed with which he passed from one scene to the next. There was, however, another side to his work on which he collaborated with nobody. Once he had defined the drama verbally, a task which was, as we shall see, of vital importance, he had to confront the musical decisions and problems. Of these we (naturally) hear little in the letters. Their documentation lies in the sketches Verdi made for his opera, which unfortunately have either been destroyed or remain unavailable.

One point which emerges with great force from the Verdi Ghislanzoni correspondence is the extent to which Verdi actually composed the libretto. At times, Ghislanzoni seems to have been little more than a versifying secretary, putting the final touches of poetic credibility to the text.

This situation was by no means unusual for Verdi. Although he never took complete responsibility for a libretto — in Italy the librettist was still referred to, and regarded as, 'il poeta' and Verdi would never have presumed to usurp this basic literary pride — his most fruitful collaborations (with Piave, Somma, Cammarano, even Boito) were on the firm understanding of 'prima la musica, dopo le parole'. The following example is quite representative of the manner in which Verdi commanded the shape of the final text. He is commenting on the final scene of Act Four:

[. . .] Yesterday I told you to write eight seven-syllable lines for Radamès before the eight for Aida. These two *soli*, even with two different *cantilene*, would have more or less the same form, the same character; and here we are back to the commonplace. The French, even in their poetry set to music, sometimes use longer or shorter lines. Why couldn't we do the same? This entire scene cannot, and must not, be anything more than a scene of singing, pure and simple. A somewhat unusual verse form for Radamès would oblige me to find a melody different from those usually set to lines of seven and eight syllables and would also oblige me to change the tempo and metre in order to write Aida's *solo* (a kind of *half-aria*). Thus with a

> somewhat unusual *cantabile* for Radamès,
> another *half-aria* for Aida,
> the *dirge* of the priests,
> the *dance* of the priestesses,
> the *farewell to life* of the lovers,
> the *in pace* of Amneris,

we would form a varied and well-developed ensemble; and if I am able, musically, to tie it all together as a whole, we shall have done something good, or at least something that will not be common. Take heart then, Signor Ghislanzoni, we are approaching the harvest; or at least you are.

Now see if you can make good verses out of this jumble of rhymeless words I am sending you, as you have done with so many others.

AIDA

And here, far from any human gaze	E qui, lontana da ogni sguardo umano
. . . To die on your heart	. . . Sul tuo cor morire (A very emotional line)

RADAMÈS

To die! Innocent?	Morire! Tu innocente?
To die! So beautiful?	Morire! . . . Tu sì bella?
You, in the April of your years	Tu, negli april degli anni
To depart from life?	Lasciar la vita?
How much I loved you, no, it cannot be told!	Quant'io t'amai, no, nol può dir favella!
But my love was fatal for you.	Ma fù mortale l'amor mio per te.
To die! Innocent?	Morire! Tu innocente?
To die! So beautiful?	Morire! Tu sì bella?
See? The angel of death	Vedi? di morte l'angelo
etc. etc.	etc. etc.

Antonio Ghislanzoni 1824 — 1893 (courtesy of Ricordi & Co., Milan)

You cannot imagine what a beautiful melody can be made out of so strange a form, and how much grace is given to it by the five-syllable line coming after the three of seven, and how much variety is lent by the two twelve-syllable lines that follow. Nevertheless, it would be good for both to be either truncated or even. See if you can knock some lines out of it and preserve the . . . *tu sì bella?*, which fits the cadence so well. [. . .] (?November 13, 1870)

Ghislanzoni dutifully 'knocked some lines' together out of the unusual syllabic pattern, and sent them off to Verdi. But he had wasted his time. The composer replied:

I received the verses, which are beautiful but not at all right for me. To avoid losing time, since you took so long sending them to me, I had already written the piece to the monstrous verses I sent you. [. . .] (undated, probably second half of November 1870)

The definitive rhyming form was presumably **arranged** during another personal meeting. A glance at the libretto shows that it follows Verdi's 'monstrous verses' very closely.

As we can see from this, Verdi was anxious to avoid a mechanical adherence to traditional operatic verse forms; he wanted a text which was intimately linked to the dramatic situations and words which would stimulate him towards musical forms which were similarly free of conventional formulae. To express his intentions more clearly, Verdi coined the term *parola scenica*, the 'theatrical word' or 'scenic utterance'. In another letter to Ghislanzoni, commenting on the Act Two Aida-Amneris duet, he explains the term's practical application:

In the duet, there are some excellent things at the beginning and at the end, but it is too long and drawn out. It seems to me that the recitative could be said in fewer lines. The strophes are good until *a te in cor destò*. But then, when the action warms up, it seems to me that the *theatrical word* is missing. I don't know if I make myself clear when I say *"theatrical word"* but I mean the word that clarifies and presents the situation neatly and plainly.

For example, the lines:

Look straight into my eyes	*In volto gli occhi affisami*
And lie again if you dare:	*E menti ancor se l'osi:*
Radamès lives . . .	*Radamès vive . . .*

This is less theatrical than the words (ugly, if you wish):

. . . with one word	*. . . con una parola*
I will tear out your secret.	*stapperò il tuo segreto.*
Look at me, I have deceived you:	*Guardami, t'ho ingannata:*
Radamès lives . . .	*Radamès vive . . .*

performance was that it allowed Verdi to spend much more than usual time and effort preparing the opera for the stage. He decided very early on not to go to Cairo for the world première (he was 'afraid of being mummified'), and concentrated his energies on the Italian première at La Scala, which was scheduled to take place very soon after. As usual, there were endless problems about the exact choice of singers. In particular the role of Amneris caused trouble, as Verdi wrote to Giulio Ricordi: 'the voice alone, no matter how beautiful [. . .], is not enough for that role. So-called *polished singing* matters little to me' (July 10, 1871), demands which were strikingly similar to those he requested of the first Lady Macbeth, some twenty-four years earlier. The composer also concerned himself with details of the *mise-en-scène*, and even offered his advice on how the orchestra ought to be arranged:

[. . .] The seating arrangement of the orchestra is of much greater importance than is commonly believed — for the *blending* of the instruments, for the sonority, and for the effect. These small improvements will afterward open the way for other innovations, which will surely come one day; among them, taking the spectators' boxes off the stage, bringing the curtain to the footlights; another, making the *orchestra invisible*. This is not my idea but Wagner's. It's excellent. It seems impossible that today we tolerate the sight of shabby *tails* and white ties, for example, mixed with Egyptian, Assyrian, and Druidic costumes, etc., etc., and, even more, the sight of the entire orchestra, which is part of the fictitious world, almost in the middle of the floor, among the whistling or applauding crowd. Add to all this the indecency of seeing the tops of the harps, the necks of the double basses, and the baton of the conductor all up in the air. [. . .] (July 10, 1871)

Verdi took an active interest in the production of his operas almost from the first, and after his experiences at the Paris Opéra in the late 1840's, never again tolerated the absurdities so common in Italian opera houses.

The Siege of Paris was lifted on January 28, 1871, but it was not until December 24 of that year that *Aida* finally received its world première at the Cairo Opera House.

On February 8, 1872, performances began at La Scala, Milan. Both productions were immediately hailed as triumphant successes, and the opera soon began the round of major European opera houses. The day after the Milanese première, Verdi summed up his achievement with characteristically blunt modesty:

[. . .] The audience reacted favourably. I don't want to affect modesty with you, but this opera is certainly not one of my worst. Time will afterward give it the place it deserves . . .
(Letter to Opprandino Arrivabene, February 9, 1872)

Gratified as he was by the enormous public success, it was not sufficient to halt his increasing disenchantment with the ways of the operatic world. The silence which had threatened after *Don Carlos* now closed in around him, apart from the *Requiem*, and no new opera came from Verdi's pen for sixteen years. In many ways, then, *Aida* marks the close of a definite period in Verdi's creative life, and for this and many other reasons, the opera is an essential experience for any who wish to understand fully the composer's artistic development.

(All the letters quoted here, and the extract from Mariette's outline, are taken from Hans Busch: Verdi's 'Aida'. The History of an Opera in Letters and Documents, Minneapolis, 1978. This fascinating book, one of the most complete collections of documents related to the history of an opera, is warmly recommended to those wishing to find out more about the genesis of Aida.)

Thematic Guide

Many of the themes from the opera have been identified in the articles by numbers in square brackets, which refer to the themes set out on these pages. The themes are also identified by the numbers in brackets at the corresponding points in the libretto, so that the words can be related to the musical themes.

[6] KING
Allegro maestoso

Now go for-ward no - ble ar - my, guard the shores of sa - cred Nile;
Su! del Ni - lo al sa - cro. li - do ac - cor - re - te, Egi - zii e - roi,

[7] AIDA
Allegro agitato

A con - que - ror re - turn!
Ri - tor - na vin - ci - tor!

[8] AIDA
Allegro giusto poco agitato

The sa - cred names of a fa - ther and lov - er
triste e dolce I sa - cri no - mi di pa - dre, d'a - mante

[9] AIDA
Cantabile

Hear me ye Gods, pi —— ty my cry!
Nu — mi, pie - tà del mio sof - frir!

[10] HIGH PRIESTESS
Andante

Al — migh — ty, al - migh - ty Phthà!
Pos - sen - te, pos - sen - te Fthà!

[11] DANCE OF THE PRIESTESSES
Allegretto

dolcissimo

[12] RAMFIS
Grave cantabile

Great God - head we pe - ti - tion thee,
Nu - me, cus - to - de e vin - di - ce

42

[13] CHORUS
Allegro giusto

We hear, ——————— the hymns and cheering
Chi mai, ——————— fra gl'inni e i plau - si

We hear, the hymns, we hear the cheer - ing,
Chi mai, chi mai fra gl'in – ni e i plau - si

[14] AMNERIS
Allegro giusto *con espansione*

Ah come — — to me, ah come my love, en - slave me
Ah! vie – — — ni, vie - ni a – mor mio, m'i - neb - bria

[15] DANCE OF THE MOORISH SLAVES
Molto allegro
pp legerissimo

[16]
Andante espressivo

[17] AIDA
Adagio cantabile

But look with pi - ty on my dis - tress
Pie - tà ti pren - da del mio do - lor

[18] AMNERIS
Adagio

I will des - troy you, I'll break your heart ——
Tre - ma, vil schia - — - va! spez - za il tuo co - re

[19] CHORUS
Maestoso

Glo - ry to I - sis, god - dess fair,
Glo - ria all' Eg – it - to ad I - si - de

43

[20] **TRIUMPHAL MARCH AND DANCES**

Maestoso

mf

[21] **Mosso**

p staccato

[22] **Mosso**

pp

[23] AMONASRO

Andante

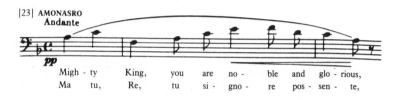

pp

Migh - ty King, you are no - ble and glo - rious,
Ma tu, Re, tu si - gno - re pos - sen - te,

[24] PRIESTS

Andante mosso

Death, O King, —— to these sav - age in - vad - ers,
Strug - gi, O Re, —— que - ste ciur - me fe - ro - ci,

[25] AIDA

Andante cantabile

sfumato

pp Oh, skies of blue, oh soft car - ess - ing bree —— zes,
O cie - li az - zur - ri, o dol - ci au - re na - ti - ve,

[26] AMONASRO

Allegro giusto *cantabile dolcissimo*

p

Once a - gain you will see our lof - ty for - ests,
Ri - ve - drai le fo - re - ste im - bal - sa - ma - te,

44

[27] AMONASRO
Allegro con impeto selvaggio

Des - troy _____ us, you ar - mies of E - gypt,
Su dun - _____ que! sor - get - te e - gi - zie co -

des - troy us! re - duce all our cities to ash - es and dust.
or - ti! col fuo - co strug - ge - te le no - stre cit - tà.

[28] AMONASRO
Andante sostenuto

Think — how your peo - ple all have been sub - jec - ted,
Pen - sa che un po - - po - lo, vin - to, stra - zia - to,

[29] RADAMÈS
Allegro giusto con trasporto — 3 —   3 —   3

At last I see _____ you, swee - test A - i - da
Pur ti ri - veg - go, mia dol - ce A - i - da

[30] AIDA
Andantino dolcissimo 3

There, where — the vir - gin for - ests - rise
Là, tra — fo - re - ste ver - gi - ni

[31] RADAMÈS
Allegro assai vivo

Hand in hand we'll fly to geth - er, find a path - way a - cross the de - sert:
Sì: fug - giam da que - ste mu - ra, al de - ser - to in - siem fug - gia - mo:

[32] AMNERIS
Andante sostenuto 3

Soon — all the priests will ga - ther here,
Già i — sa - cer - do - ti a - du - nan - si

45

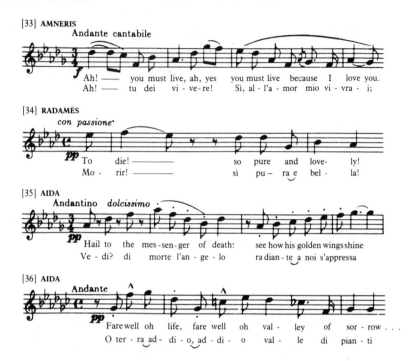

[33] **AMNERIS**
Andante cantabile

Ah! —— you must live, ah, yes you must live because I love you.
Ah! —— tu dei vi - ve - re! Sì, al - l'a - mor mio vi - vra - i;

[34] **RADAMÈS**
con passione

pp To die! —————— so pure and love- ly!
Mo - rir! —————— sì pu — ra e bel - la!

[35] **AIDA**
Andantino dolcissimo

pp Hail to the mes -sen-ger of death: see how his golden wings shine
Ve - di? di morte l'an - ge - lo ra dian - te a noi s'appressa

[36] **AIDA**
Andante

pp Farewell oh life, fare well oh val - ley of sor - row . . .
O ter - ra ad - di - o, ad - di - o val - le di pian - ti

46

Aida

an opera in four acts by Giuseppe Verdi

Libretto by Antonio Ghislanzoni based on a story by Auguste Mariette
English version by Edmund Tracey

This is the performing version used by English National Opera at the London Coliseum. Ghislanzoni's libretto is written in verse, laid out here correctly as far as possibly; in several cases, this was altered by Verdi in the course of composing the opera, and so these amendments interrupt the original scheme of alignment. Where choruses and ensembles repeat lines, this has been indicated also, to make it easy to follow the text as it is sung.

The stage directions and character descriptions are those in the original full score and do not necessarily represent the ENO (or any other) production. They have been followed because they were sanctioned by the composer and consequently illustrate his intentions, and form a more or less integral part of the text. The titles of musical pieces follow the relevant scene descriptions after an oblique and the numbers in square brackets refer to the thematic guide.

The first performance of *Aida* was given at the Cairo Opera House on December 24, 1871. The first performance in London was at Covent Garden on June 22, 1876. The first performance in the USA was at the New York Academy of Music on November 26, 1873. It was first performed by Sadler's Wells Opera on March 20, 1931, and by English National Opera at the London Coliseum on September 26, 1979.

Ramfis *high priest*	bass
Radamès *captain of the guard*	tenor
Amneris *princess of Egypt*	mezzo-soprano
Aida *an Ethiopian slave*	soprano
The King of Egypt	bass
Messenger	tenor
High priestess	soprano
Amonasro *Aida's father, king of Ethiopia*	baritone

Priests, priestesses, ministers, officers, guards, courtiers, Nubians, populace, slaves, prisoners

Act One

Scene One. *Hall in the palace of the King at Memphis. To the right and left a colonnade with statues and flowering shrubs. At the back a grand gate from which may be seen the temples and palaces of Memphis and the Pyramids. | Introduction. Radames and Ramfis in consultation*

RAMFIS

Yes, Ethiopia once again has dared to Defy our power: On the Nile we are threaten'd And in the state of Thebes. I sent a messenger To find the truth.	Sì: corre voce che l'Etiope ardisca Sfidarci ancora, e del Nilo la valle E Tebe minacciar. Fra breve un messo Recherà il ver.

RADAMÈS

The will of Isis has been consulted?	La sacra Iside consultasti?

RAMFIS

She has decided Who will take the supreme Command of all our armies.	Ella ha nomato Dell'Egizie falangi Il condottier supremo.

RADAMÈS

Ah, what an honour!	Oh lui felice!

RAMFIS
(meaningfully, looking fixedly at Radamès)

Nobly born, he's young and valiant. The god has spoken: Now I must tell the King.	Giovane e prode è desso. Ora, del Nume Reco i decreti al Re.

Ramfis leaves. | Romanza

RADAMÈS

I pray that I Be chosen and achieve my Dream of Glory! With a glorious valiant army And I as leader . . . Egypt victorious, . . acclaimed By the whole of Memphis! To you my sweet Aida I'd enter crown'd with laurel . . . Saying: 'for you I battled, for you I conquer'd!'	Se quel guerrier Io fossi! se il mio sogno Si avverasse! Un esercito di prodi Da me guidato . . . e la vittoria, e il plauso Di Menfi tutta! E a te, mia dolce Aida, Tornar di lauri cinto . . . Dirti: 'per te ho pugnato, per te ho vinto!'

Goddess Aida, fair as a vision, Magic in beauty, glowing with light, Like some fair planet you shine above me, You are the ruler of my whole life. Home to your country I would return you,	[3]	Celeste Aida, forma divina, Mistico serto di luce e fior, Del mio pensiero tu sei regina, Tu di mia vita sei lo splendor. Il tuo bel cielo vorrei ridarti,

49

Back to the sweet-scented land you love:	Le dolci brezze del patrio suol;
Then with a garland I would adorn you,	Un regal serto sul crin posarti,
Build you a throne near to the sun!	Ergerti un trono vicino al sol!

Amneris enters | Duet and Trio

AMNERIS [4]

Have you just heard a joyful	Quale insolita gioia
Tale that stirs you? A valiant	Nel tuo sguardo! Di quale
Noble elation seems to glow inside you!	Nobil fierezza ti balena il volto!
How all the world would envy	Degna d'invidia oh! quanto,
And honour the woman who merely by her presence	Saria la donna il cui bramato aspetto
And her beauty could waken in you such ardour!	Tanta luce di gaudio in te destasse!

RADAMÈS

A soldier's heart beats faster	D'un sogno avventuroso
When he's dreaming of glory. Isis today	Si beava il mio cuore. Oggi, la Diva
Has named the man who will command our army	Profferse il nome del guerrier che al campo
And lead them forth to face the foe . . . Ah! if only	Le schiere egizie condurrà . . . Ah! s'io fossi
I might achieve that honour!	A tal' onor prescelto . . .

AMNERIS

Another dream may charm you,	Nè un altro sogno mai
Still more sweet, still more lovely,	Più gentil, più soave
To captivate your heart. A secret longing . . .	Al core ti parlò? Non hai tu in Menfi
A devotion . . . more tender?	Desiderii, speranze?

RADAMÈS [5]

I? (A devotion?	Io! (Quale inchiesta!
Surely she can't discover	Forse l'arcano amore
the love that burns within me?)	Scoprì che m'arde in core . . .)

AMNERIS [5]

(I'll die if there's another . . .	(Oh! guai se un altro amore
A rival holding him as lover!)	Ardesse a lui nel core!)

RADAMÈS

(Can she have guess'd Aida	(Della sua schiava il nome
By looking in my eyes?)	Mi lesse nel pensier!

AMNERIS

(I will die if I have found a	(Guai se il mio sguardo penetra
Darkly hidden secret love!)	Questo fatal mister!)

Aida enters [1]

RADAMÈS
(seeing Aida)

Aida!	Dessa!

AMNERIS
(to herself; watching)

(He is troubled . . . Ah, what a	(Ei si turba, e quale
Look of devotion there!	Sguardo rivolse a lei!

50

Aida! Is she my rival?   [5]   Aida! A me rivale . . .
Is he in love with her?)   Forse saria costei?)

(turning to Aida)

Come my dear, come close to me . . .   Vieni, o diletta appressati,
Never a slave I find you!   Schiava non sei nè ancella,
You are a sister dear to me,   Qui, dove in dolce fascino
With sweetest ties I bind you . . .   Io ti chiamai sorella . . .
Weeping? And will you share   Piangi? delle tue lacrime
With a sister the sorrow,   Svela il segreto a me.
Causing you tears of woe?

AIDA

Alas, I hear the cries of war,   Ohimè! di guerra fremere
The fearful shouts re-echo . . .   L'atroce grido io sento,
What will befall my countrymen?   Per l'infelice patria,
For them, for you, I fear so.   Per me, per voi pavento.

AMNERIS

Is this the truth? No deeper reason Favelli il ver? Nè s'agita
Causes your dismay?   Più grave cura in te?
(Aida! Beware my anger!)   (Trema, o rea schiava!)

(Aida casts down her eyes and tries to hide her emotion)

RADAMÈS
(watching Amneris)

(I see her eyes are flashing . . .   (Nel volto a lei balena . . .

AMNERIS
(aside, regarding Aida)

Aida, beware my anger!   Ah! Trema, rea schiava, trema!

RADAMÈS

With anger and suspicion . . .)   Lo sdegno ed il sospetto)

AMNERIS

In your heart I'll find the secret!   Ch'io nel tuo cor discenda!

RADAMÈS

Can she have read the secret   Guai se l'arcano affetto
Our hearts have sweetly hidden? . . A noi leggesse in cor!

AMNERIS

I mean to know the truth   Trema che il ver m'apprenda
Of your blushes and of your tears!   Quel pianto e quel rossor!

RADAMÈS

Hidden inside our hearts?   Guai se leggesse in cor!

AIDA

Ah! no, sighs for my country   Ah! — no, sulla mia patria
Now vie in my heart with other sorrows, Non geme il cor soltanto;
These tears fast flowing are mourning Quello ch'io verso è pianto
A sad, unlucky love!   Di sventurato amor!

RADAMÈS

I see in her eyes an angry flash   Nel volto a lei balena

An angry flash, suspecting our love!
She reads the tender passion,
That's hidden in our hearts!

Lo sdegno ed il sospetto.
Guai se l'arcano affetto
A noi leggesse in cor!

AMNERIS

Oh slave, beware my anger,
For in your heart I'll find the truth!
I mean to know the truth about your blushes,
Your blushes and all your tears!

Rea schiava, trema!
Ch'io nel tuo cor discenda!
Ah! trema che il ver m'apprenda

Quel pianto e quel rossor!

The King enters, preceded by his guard and followed by Ramfis, ministers, priests, officers, etc. | Scena and Concerted Piece

THE KING

Grave is the cause that
Summons round their King the faithful men of Egypt.
From the Ethiopian front a messenger
Has just been admitted. Grave is the news he brings us.
So we must hear him . . .

Alta cagion v'aduna,
O fidi Egizii, al vostro Re d'intorno.

Dai confin d'Etiopia un messaggiero
Dianzi giungea, gravi novelle ei reca.

Vi piaccia udirlo . . .

(to an official)

Now bring him here before us!

Il messaggier s'avanzi!

The Messenger enters.

THE MESSENGER

Our sacred land has been defiled by fierce
Ethiopian invaders . . . They ravaged all our
Fields and our farmsteads, burnt all our harvests . . . embolden'd
By so easy a triumph, the savage troops
Are advancing on the city.

Il sacro suolo dell'Egitto è invaso
Dai barbari Etiopi. I nostri campi

Fur devastati, arse le messi, e baldi

Della facil vittoria, i predatori
Già marciano su Tebe.

ALL

They would not dare to!

Ed osan tanto!

THE MESSENGER

They are led by a warrior as savage
As a tiger — Amonasro.

Un guerriero indomabile, feroce,
Li conduce — Amonasro.

ALL

The King!

Il Re!

AIDA
(aside)

(My father!)

(Mio padre!)

THE MESSENGER

Now Thebes has risen; from ev'ry door and gateway
Our men are rushing forth hurling
Fire and sword upon the wild invader.

Già Tebe è in armi e dalle cento porte

Sul barbaro invasore
Proromperà, guerra recando e morte.

THE KING

Let death and battle be our only warcry!	Sì, guerra e morte il nostro grido sia!

ALL

Battle! Battle!	Guerra! guerra!
Destruction, no quarter given!	Tremenda, inesorata!

THE KING

(addressing Radamès)

Holiest Goddess Isis	Iside venerata
Has chosen her commander,	Di nostre schiere invitte
The man to lead our glorious troops to battle.	Già designava il condottier supremo:
Radamès!	Radamès!

ALL

Radamès!	Radamès!

RADAMÈS

Ah! My thanks to Heaven.	Ah! sien grazie ai Numi!
My prayers have been heard!	Son paghi i voti miei!

AMNERIS

Our leader! our leader!	Ei duce! ei duce!

AIDA

I'm frightened, I'm frightened!	Io tremo! Io tremo!

THE KING

Go now to Vulcan's temple	Or di Vulcano al tempio
Brave Radamès, to gird	Muovi, O guerrier; le sacre
On the armour of victorious Egypt!	Armi ti cingi e alla vittoria vola.

Now go forward noble army,	[6]	Su! del Nilo al sacro lido
Guard the shores of sacred Nile;		Accorrete, Egizii eroi;
Ev'ry voice proclaim our warcry:		D'ogni cor proprompa il grido:
Death and destruction fall upon the foe!		Guerra e morte, morte allo stranier!

RAMFIS

Glory to Isis! All bow before her!	Gloria ai Numi! ognun rammenti
She it is who guides our fortunes.	Ch'essi reggono gli eventi,
Great her might high in the heavens;	Che in poter dei Numi solo
Isis rules the world below.	Stan le sorti del guerrier.

Bow down in homage! Great the might of Isis.	Ognun rammenti
She guides our fortune,	Che in poter dei Numi, dei Numi solo
Isis rules the world below!	Stan le sorti del guerrier!

MINISTERS, CAPTAINS

Now go forward noble army	Su! del Nilo al sacro lido
We shall form a human barrier;	Sien barriera i nostri petti;
Ev'ry voice proclaim our warcry:	Non echeggi che un sol grido;
Death and destruction fall upon the foe!	Guerra, guerra e morte allo stranier!

THE KING

Yes, now go forward noble army,	Su! su! del Nilo al sacro lido
Hasten forward to the river.	Accorrete, Egizii eroi;

Let ev'ry voice proclaim the cry	Da ogni cor prorompa un grido:
Destruction fall upon the foe!	Guerra e morte allo stranier!

AIDA
(to herself)

Who can tell me who I weep for, who I pray for?	Per chi piango? Per chi prego?
Ah this fatal pow'r that binds me!	Qual poter m'avvince a lui!
Dare I love him, yes, love him	Deggio amarlo ed è costui
Both a stranger and a foe!	Un nemico, uno stranier!

RADAMÈS

I can feel the flame of glory	Sacro fremito di gloria
Fire my mind and quite consume me!	Tutta l'anima m'investe.
We will fight and we will conquer:	Su! corriamo alla vittoria!
Death and destruction fall upon the foe!	Guerra e morte allo stranier!

AMNERIS
(handing a standard to Radamès)

From my hand, oh noble leader,	Di mia man ricevi, o duce,
Take this standard bright with glory;	Il vessillo glorioso;
May it guide you, long may it light you	Ti sia guida, ti sia luce
On the valiant path you go!	Della gloria sul sentier.

THE KING [6]

Now go forward, noble army *(etc.)*	Su! del Nilo al sacro lido, *(etc.)*

RAMFIS

Bow in homage men of Egypt!	Gloria ai Numi, e ognun rammenti
Mighty Isis guides our fortunes:	Ch'essi regono gli eventi,
Hers the might and hers the glory!	Che in poter de' Numi solo
Holy Isis rules the world below!	Stan le sorti, le sorti del guerrier!

RADAMÈS, MESSENGER

Fight and conquer!	Su! corriamo,
Fight and we will be victorious!	Su! corriamo alla vittoria!

MINISTERS, CAPTAINS

Now go forward, noble army,	Su! del Nilo al sacro lido
We shall form a human barrier *(etc.)*	Sien barriera i nostri petti, *(etc.)*

AMNERIS

I pray it guide you	. . . ti sia guida
May it guide you, may it light you,	Ti sia guida, ti sia luce
Yes, may it light you on the valiant path you go.	Della gloria sul sentier.

AIDA

(Who can tell me who I weep for, *(etc.)*	(Per chi piango? Per chi prego?, *(etc.)*

ALL
(except Aida)

Battle! Battle! Battle!	Guerra! guerra! guerra!
Destroy them! Death and vengeance on the foe!	Sterminio all'invasor!

AIDA

Dare I give him my heart and love	Deggio amarlo, e veggio in lui
Both a stranger and a foe? Ah!	Un nemico, uno stranier! Ah!

54

A conqueror return!   Ritorna vincitor!

A conqueror return!   Ritorna vincitor!

Exeunt all but Aida.| Scena and Romanza

A conqueror return! How can I utter   Ritorna vincitor! E dal mio labbro
Words full of betrayal? Do I wish   Uscì l'empia parola! Vincitor
My father conquer'd, a man who wages   Del padre mio, di lui che impugna l'armi
    war just
For me, just to restore me   Per me, per ridonarmi
My homeland, my palace, the royal name   Una patria, una reggia, e il nome illustre
I am forc'd to keep unspoken? Do I pray   Che qui celar m'è forza! Vincitor
He kill my brothers? . . I think I see   De' miei fratelli . . . ond'io lo vegga,
    him, stain'd   tinto
With the blood I cherish, hoisted high in   Del sangue amato, trionfar nel plauso
    triumph
By Egyptian battalions. Behind his   Dell'Egizie coorti! E dietro il carro,
    chariot,
A King, my father, led in chains of   Un Re, mio padre, di catene avvinto!
    bondage!

Oh Heaven, forgive all   L'insana parola,
The mad words I utter!   O Numi, sperdete!
Restore to a loving   Al seno d'un padre
Father his daughter;   La figlia rendete;
And slaughter the armies   Struggete le squadre
That so oppress our land! Ah! —   Dei nostri oppressor! Ah! —
Wretched folly to say so! My own   Sventurata! che dissi? E l'amor mio?
    beloved!
How could I turn against him,   Dunque scordar poss'io
With his fervent devotion when all   Questo fervido amore che, oppressa e
    turn'd from me: schiava,
His smile was like the sun shining upon   Come raggio di sol qui mi beava?
    me.
Shall I invoke the death   Imprecherò la morte
Of Radamès, the man I love so dearly?   A Radamès, a lui ch'amo pur tanto!
Ah, shall I ever bear   Ah! non fu in terra mai
This cruel, deadly weight of burning   Da più crudeli angoscie un core affranto!
    sorrow?

The sacred names of a father and   [8]   I sacri nomi di padre, d'amante
    lover
Are what I must not cherish nor even   Nè profferir poss'io, nè ricordar . . .
    say . . .
Confused and trembling . . . the one and   Per l'un, per l'altro . . . confusa e
    the other . . .   tremante . . .
I only want to weep . . . I want to pray.   Io piangere vorrei, vorrei pregar.
Is it a crime now to own such a feeling,   Ma la mia prece in bestemmia si
                                                 muta . . .
And am I wrong to weep and wrong to   Delitto e il pianto a me, colpa il sospir . . .
    sigh?
In darkest night all my senses are reeling, In notte cupa la mente e perduta,
In aching distress I long to die!   E nell'ansia crudel vorrei morir.

Hear me ye Gods, pity my cry! [9]	Numi, pietà del mio soffrir!
All hope is gone, joy comes no more.	Speme non v'ha pel mio dolor.
Ah, fatal love, ah, mighty love,	Amor fatal, tremendo amor,
Come, break my heart, leave me to die!	Spezzami il cor, fammi morir!

Scene Two. *Interior of the Temple of Vulcan at Memphis. A mysterious light from above. A long row of columns, one behind the other, vanishing in darkness. Statues of various deities. In the middle of the stage, above a platform covered with carpet, rises the altar surmounted with sacred emblems. Golden tripods emitting fumes of incense.*/ *Grand Scene of the Consecration and First Finale*

HIGH PRIESTESS
[10] *alone*

Almighty, almighty Phtha, the breathing	Possente, possente Ftha, del mondo
Spirit of life in us all, ah!	Spirito animator, ah!

(with chorus of priestesses from within)

We here implore thee!	Noi t'invochiamo!

RAMFIS, PRIESTS

Who, from the void, created	Tu che dal nulla hai tratto
Sea, air and earth and sky,	L'onde, la terra, il ciel,
We here implore thee!	Noi t'invochiamo!

HIGH PRIESTESS

Almighty, almighty Phtha, the fruitful	Immenso, immenso Fthà, del mondo
Spirit of life in us all, ah! ah!	Spirito fecondator, ah! ah!

(with priestesses)

We here implore thee!	Noi t'invochiamo!

RAMFIS, PRIESTS

Lord God of ancient mystery,	Nume che del tuo spirito
Who art both son and sire,	Sei figlio e genitor,
We here implore thee!	Noi t'invochiamo!

HIGH PRIESTESS

Fire uncreated beyond all time,	Fuoco increato, eterno,
Whence came the light and sun! ah, ah!	Onde ebbe luce il sol, ah, ah!

(with Priestesses)

We here implore thee!	Noi t'invochiamo!

RAMFIS, PRIESTS

Life spirit universal,	Vita dell'universo,
Great fount of deathless love,	Mito d'eterno amor,
We here implore!	Noi t'invochiam!

PRIESTESSES

Almighty Phtha!	Immenso Ftha!

RAMFIS, PRIESTS

We here implore!	Noi t'invochiam!

Sacred Dance of the Priestesses [11]. *Radamès, unarmed, is brought into the Temple and conducted to the altar. A silver veil is placed on his head.*

PRIESTESSES

Almighty Phtha!	Immenso Fthà!

56

RAMFIS, PRIESTS

We here implore!   Noi t'invochiam!

RAMFIS
(to Radamès)

The gods have shown you favour: to you they now   Mortal, diletto ai Numi, a te fidate

Entrust the future of Egypt. The sacred sword   Son d'Egitto le sorti. Il sacro brando

Of the god will serve you, striking the invaders   Dal Dio temprato, per tua man diventi

And spreading dismay, massacre, carnage.   Ai nemici terror, folgore, morte.

PRIESTS

The sacred sword   Il sacro brando

Of the god will serve you, striking the invaders   Dal Dio temprato, per tua man diventi

And spreading dismay, massacre, carnage.   Ai nemici terror, folgore, morte.

RAMFIS

Massacre, carnage.   Folgore, morte.
(to the god)

Great Godhead we petition thee,   [12] Nume, custode e vindice
Great guardian and avenger,   Di questa sacra terra,
Come, raise thy hand in blessing,   La mano tua distendi
Blessing over Egyptian soil.   Sovra l'egizio suol.

RADAMÈS

Great Godhead we petition thee,   Nume, che duce ed arbitro
Great judge and holy leader.   Sei d'ogni umana guerra,
Come grant us thy protection,   Proteggi tu, difendi
Save us, protect Egyptian soil.   D'Egitto il sacro suol.

RAMFIS

Grant us they blessing.   La mano tua,
Come raise thy hand in blessing   La mano tua distendi
Over our holy Egyptian soil.   Sovra l'egizio suol.

PRIESTS

Great Godhead we petition thee,   Nume, custode e vindice
Our guardian and avenger,   Di questa sacra terra,
Come raise thy hand in blessing   La mano tua distendi
Blessing over Egyptian soil!   Sovra l'egizio suol!

RAMFIS

Great Godhead we petition thee,   Nume, custode ed arbitro
Our guardian and avenger,   Di questa sacra terra,
Come raise thy hand in blessing   La mano tua distendi
Blessing over Egyptian soil!   Sovra l'egizio suol!

RADAMÈS

Come, grant us aid, protect us and defend us.   Proteggi tu, difendi

Protect our holy Egyptian soil!   D'Egitto il sacro suol!

PRIESTESSES

Almighty, almighty Phtha.   Possente, possente Fthà.

Almighty Phtha.   Possente Fthà.

Life spirit in us all.   Del mondo creator.

Life spirit in us all,   Spirto fecondator
Who hast from nothing the world   Tu che dal nulla hai tratto
Created,   Il mondo,
Thou who from nothing waves hast   Tu che dal nulla hai tratto
Created, earth, air and Heaven,   L'onde, la terra, il cielo,
We here implore thee!   Noi t'invochiamo!

Ah! — Ah!   Ah! — Ah!
Almighty Phtha!   Possente Fthà!
Breathing spirit of life in all,   Spirito animator,
Fruitful spirit of life in all.   Spirito fecondator.

We here implore!   Noi t'invochiam!

Almighty Phtha!   Immenso Fthà!

We here implore!   Noi t'invochiam!

Almighty Phtha!   Immenso Fthà!

Almighty Phtha!   Immenso Fthà!

Act Two

Scene One. *A hall in the apartments of Amneris. Amneris surrounded by female slaves who attire her for the triumphal feast. Tripods emitting perfumed vapours. Young Moorish slaves waving feather fans.| Introduction . Scena, Chorus of Women and Dance of Moorish slaves.*

SLAVE-GIRLS [13]

We hear the hymns and cheering,	Chi mai fra gl'inni e i plausi
Praising all his glory and fame;	Erge alla gloria il vol,
His gaze is fierce and terrible,	Al par d'un Dio terribile,
He shines in our acclaim.	Fulgente al par del sol!
Let sweetest flowers rain on you,	Vieni, sul crin ti piovano
Competing with laurels around your brow;	Contesti ai lauri i fior;
Let songs of glory celebrate	Suonin di gloria i cantici
Your lover's tender vow.	Coi cantici d'amor.

AMNERIS [14]

Ah come to me, ah come my love, enslave me,	(Ah! Vieni, vieni amor mio, m'inebbria,
Inflame my heart with love.	Fammi beato il cor.)

SLAVE-GIRLS [13]

The hordes of fierce barbarians,	Or, dove son le barbare
All have vanished away.	Orde dello stranier?
Like sunlight melting winter snows,	Siccome nebbia sparvero
Our armies won the day.	Al soffio del guerrier.
A victory resounding	Vieni: di gloria il premio
Has won our hero fame and glorious high reward.	Raccogli, o vincitor;
And after deeds of glory	T'arrise la vittoria,
The voice of love is heard.	T'arriderà l'amor.

AMNERIS [14]

Ah come to me, ah come, my love awaken me	(Ah! Vieni, vieni amor mio, ravvivami
And speak a tender word!	D'un caro accento ancor!)

Dance of the young Moorish slaves [15]. The slaves continue attiring Amneris.

SLAVE-GIRLS [13]

Let sweetest flowers rain on you *(etc.)*	Vieni: sul crin ti piovano *(etc.)*

AMNERIS [14]

Ah come to me, ah come my love, enslave me, *(etc.)*	Ah! Vieni, vieni amor mio m'inebbria, *(etc.)*
No more now! Aida makes her way toward us . . .	Silenzio! Aida verso noi s'avanza . . .
Child of the conquer'd, to me her grief is sacred.	Figlia de' vinti, il suo dolor m'e sacro.

At a sign from Amneris, the slaves retire. Aida enters, carrying the crown.

But when I see her, suspicious	Nel rivederla, il dubbio
Fears come back to plague me . . .	Atroce in me si desta . . .
I'll discover the secret she is hiding!	Il mistero fatal si squarci alfine!

Scena and Duet

(to Aida with feigned affection)

Now the battle is over your people suffer,	Fu la sorte dell'armi a' tuoi funesta,
Wretched Aida! The sorrow	Povera Aida! Il lutto
That oppresses your heart may I not share it?	Che ti pesa sul cor teco divido.
Accept the hand of friendship . . .	Io son l'amica tua . . .
Nothing shall be denied you . . . Live and be happy!	Tutto da me tu avrai . . . Vivrai felice!

AIDA

Be happy! Ah, how can I,	Felice esser poss'io
So far from all my people, hearing no word about	Lungi dal suol natio, qui dove ignota
The fate of my father and my brothers?	M'è la sorte del padre e dei fratelli?

AMNERIS

Ah, how you grieve me! All human misfortune	Ben ti compiango! pure hanno un confine
Must sometime have an end . . . Time will bring comfort	I mali di quaggiù . . . Sanerà il tempo
And heal your present misery . . .	Le angoscie del tuo core . . .
Greater than time too, a god more mighty . . . the god of love.	E più che il tempo, un Dio possente . . . amore!

AIDA [1]
(much moved, aside)

Ah, love, ah, love, oh, joy and torment . . .	Amore, amore! gaudio, tormento . . .
Sweetest elation, burning despair . . .	Soave ebbrezza, ansia crudel . . .
In your affliction I feel life quicken . . .	Ne' tuoi dolori la vita io sento,
A smile from you can open Heaven's gate.	Un tuo sorriso mi schiude il ciel.

AMNERIS
(to herself)

Ev'ry expression . . . all this excitement	Ah, quel pallore, quel turbamento
Tell of the secret fever of love . . .	Svelan l'arcana febbre d'amor . . .
Have I the courage? Dare I still ask her?	D'interrogarla quasi ho sgomento,
I share the torments of all her alarm.	Divido l'ansie del suo terror.

[16] *(to Aida, eyeing her fixedly)*

But now a new anxiety Assails you, sweet Aida?	Ebben: qual nuovo fremito T'assal, gentil Aida?
Come share your secret thoughts with me,	I tuoi segreti svelami,
Trust in my friendship, my love and understanding.	All'amor mio t'affida.
Among the men who went to war Fighting against your country . . .	Tra i forti che pugnarono Della tua patria a danno . . .
It may be that one has kindled Longing in your secret heart?	Qualcuno un dolce affanno Forse a te in cor destò?

A longing? Che parli?

AMNERIS [16]

A cruel destiny A tutti barbara
Came only to a few men . . . Non si mostrò la sorte
For though our glorious Radamès Se in campo il duce impavido
Has met his death in battle . . . Cadde trafitto a morte . . .

AIDA

You cannot mean it! Radamès! Che mai dicesti! misera!

AMNERIS

Yes, Radamès was killed Sì, Radamès da' tuoi
In battle . . . Fu spento . . .

AIDA

Wretched fate! Misera!

AMNERIS

How can you mourn him? E pianger puoi?

AIDA

I'll mourn him for evermore! Per sempre io piangerò!

AMNERIS

The gods now have avenged you . . . Gli Dei t'han vendicata . . .

AIDA

The gods have always Avversi sempre
Denied me what I wanted . . . A me furo i Numi . . .

AMNERIS
(*breaking out in anger*)

Fear me! I know your secret . . . Trema! in cor ti lessi . . .
You love him . . . Tu l'ami . . .

AIDA

Love him! Io!

AMNERIS

Don't deny it! Non mentire!
But one word further: the truth will Un detto ancora e il vero
Be clear . . . Look in my eyes now . . . Saprò. Fissami in volto . . .
I meant to trap you . . . Radamès is Io t'ingannavo . . . Radamès vive . . .
living . . .

AIDA
(*falling to her knees, in exaltation*)

Living! Vive!
Gods I thank you! Ah, grazie o Numi!

AMNERIS

And still you would deceive me? E ancor mentir tu speri?
Yes . . . you love him . . . I love him Sì, tu l'ami . . . Ma l'amo . . .
too . . .

(*with utmost fury*)

| You understand? You see your rival . . . | Anch'io, intendi tu? son tua rivale, |
| I who am Pharaoh's daughter. | Figlia de' Faraoni! |

AIDA

(drawing herself up with pride)

| You my rival . . . | Mia rivale! |
| Well then so be it . . . I too . . . could be . . . | Ebben sia pure . . . anch'io . . . son tal . . . |

(checking herself and falling at the feet of Amneris)

| What have I said? Forgive! Forgive me! Ah! | Ah! che dissi mai? pietà! perdono! ah! |

[17]

But look with pity on my distress . . .	Pietà ti prenda del mio dolor . . .
It's true I adore him with all my heart . . .	E vero, io l'amo d'immenso amor . . .
Ah, you are happy and you are mighty,	Tu sei felice, tu sei possente,
I live alone for one glance of love!	Io vivo solo per questo amor!

AMNERIS [18]

I will destroy you, I'll break your heart . . .	Trema, vil schiava! spezza il tuo core . . .
Daring to love him could mean your downfall.	Segnar tua morte puo quest'amore.
Mine is the power ruling your future,	Del tuo destino arbitra sono,
Hatred and vengeance now rule in my heart.	D'odio e vendetta le furie ho in cor!

AIDA

Ah! you are happy and you are mighty . . .	Tu sei felice, tu sei possente,
I live alone for one glance of love!	Io vivo solo per quest'amor!
Ah look with pity on my distress . . . *(etc.)*	Pietà ti prenda del mio dolor! *(etc.)*

AMNERIS

Fear me Aida!	Trema, vil schiava!
I'll break your heart in pieces, you slave girl!	Spezza il tuo cor, trema vil schiava!
I hold your future in my hand	Del tuo destino arbitra io son,
And hate and vengeance now rule in my heart *(etc.)*	D'odio e vendetta le furie ho in cor! *(etc.)*

CHORUS

(outside)

Now go forward noble army,	Su! del Nilo al sacro lido
Guard the Nile, our sacred river;	Sien barriera i nostri petti;
Ev'ry voice proclaim our warcry:	Non echeggi che un sol grido:
Death and destruction fall upon the foe!	Guerra e morte allo stranier!

AMNERIS

To the triumph now preparing	Alla pompa che s'appresta,
You, Aida, will attend me;	Meco, o schiava, assisterai;
You prostrated in the dust and I,	Tu prostrata nella polvere,
I enthron'd beside the King.	Io sul trono accanto al Re.

AIDA

Ah, have pity, what is left me,	Ah, pietà! che piu mi resta?
My whole life is now a desert;	Un deserto è la mia vita;
Live and reign in highest glory,	Vivi e regna, il tuo furore

I will learn to calm your rage.	Io tra breve placherò.
This fond love that so annoys you	Quest'amore che t'irrita
Soon will perish in the grave.	Nella tomba spegnerò.

AMNERIS

Follow behind me and I will show you	Vien . . . mi segui, apprenderai
What it means —	Se lottar –

AIDA

Ah, no more!	Ah! pietà!

AMNERIS

— to compete with me.	— tu puoi con me,
What it means to compete with me.	Se lottar tu puoi con me.

AIDA

Ah, no more,	Quest'amor
This love will perish within the grave.	Nella tomba io spegnerò.
No more! no more!	Pietà! Pietà!

AMNERIS

Ah, what it means	Apprenderai
To compete with me.	Se lottar tu puoi con me,
Come, attend me —	Vieni, mi segui —

CHORUS
(outside) [6]

Let destruction strike the foe!	Guerra e morte allo stranier!

AMNERIS

— and I will show you	— e apprenderai
What it means to compete with me.	Se lottar tu puoi con me.

CHORUS

Let destruction strike the foe!	Guerra e morte allo stranier!

Exit Amneris.

AIDA [9]

Hear me, ye gods, pity my cry!	Numi, pietà del mio martir,
All hope is gone and joy comes no more.	Speme non v'ha pel mio dolor . . .
Hear me ye gods, ah, hear my prayer!	Numi, pietà del mio soffrir,
Ah, hear my prayer, ah, hear my prayer!	Numi, pietà! Pietà! Pietà!

Scene Two. *An avenue to the City of Thebes. In front a clump of palms. On the right a temple dedicated to Ammon. On the left a throne with a purple canopy. At the back a triumphal arch. The stage is crowded with people. | Grand Finale Two.*

Enter the King followed by the Court — officers, priests, captains, fan bearers, standard bearers. Afterwards Amneris with Aida and slaves. The King takes his seat on the throne. Amneris places herself at his left hand.

POPULACE [19]

Glory to Isis, goddess fair,	Gloria al'Egitto, ad Iside
You who protect and shelter.	Che il sacro suol protegge!
Our King who rules the Delta,	Al Re che il Delta regge
Praise we in festive song!	Inni festosi alziam!

Glory! Glory! Glory!   Gloria! gloria! gloria!
Glory oh King!   Gloria al Re!

WOMEN

The lotus buds and laurel   S'intrecci il loto al lauro
Entwine in fragrant bowers!   Sul crin dei vincitori!
A cloud of summer flowers   Nembo gentil di fiori
Hides all the swords in a veil. Stenda sull'armi un vel.
Now dance Egyptian maidens   Danziam, fanciulle egizie,
To music sweet and holy,   Le mistiche carole,
Dance fervently and slowly,   Come d'intorno al sole
Honour the leader we hail.   Danzano gli astri in ciel.

PRIESTS [2]

All praise and glory to mighty gods   Della vittoria agl'arbitri
In Heaven; now bow down before them;   Supremi il guardo ergete;
Worship and adore them   Grazie agli Dei rendete
On this most blessed day.   Nel fortunato dì.

POPULACE
(women)

Dance fervently and slowly,   Come d'intorno al sole
Honour the leader we hail!   Danzano gli astri in ciel.

(men)

Praise we in festive song,   Inni festosi alziam al Re,
We praise our King in festive song!   Alziamo al Re.

PRIESTS

Worship, bow down before them   Grazie agli Dei rendete
On this most blessed day.   Nel fortunato dì.

The Egyptian troops march past the King [20]; *then dancing girls with the spoil captured from the Ethiopians.* | *Ballabile* [21, 22]

POPULACE [19]

Glorious warrior Radamès,   Vieni, o guerriero vindice,
Conqueror of our foes;   Vieni a gioir con noi;
We strew before our heroes,   Sul passo degli eroi
Laurel and fragrant bay!   I lauri, i fior versiam!

PRIESTS

The gods are everlasting,   Agli arbitri supremi
Bow down before them,   Il guardo ergete;
Worship the gods and adore them Grazie agli Dei rendete
On this most blessed day.   Nel fortunato dì.

Radames enters.

POPULACE
(sopranos)

Hail Radamès!   Vieni, o guerrier,
Praise him, let all rejoice,   Vieni a gioir con noi,
Hail Radamès, victor of all our foes,   Sul passo degl'eroi
We strew before the heroes   I lauri, i fior versiam.
Laurels twin'd with bay.
Hail glorious warrior, victor of all our
  foes.

Glory, glory, glory,	Gloria, gloria, gloria,
Hail Radamès! Praise him,	Gloria al guerrier, vieni,
Praise him glorious hero!	Vieni a gioir con noi,
Hail Radamès, victor of all our foes.	Sul passo degl'eroi
We strew before the heroes	I lauri, i fior versiam.
Laurels twin'd with bay.	

PRIESTS

Worship, worship, worship,	Grazie, grazie, grazie,
Worship the gods,	Grazie agli Dei rendete,
Give them praise and glory!	Nel fortunato dì.
Worship the gods and sing their praise.	
Adore them, adore the gods and praise them.	

POPULACE

Glory! glory! glory!	Gloria! gloria! gloria!
Glory to Egypt!	Gloria all'Egitto, gloria!

The King descends from the throne to embrace Radamès.

THE KING

Valiant pride of your country, I here salute you.	Salvator della patria, io ti saluto.
Hero, see, my daughter is at hand to greet you	Vieni, e mia figlia di sua man ti porga
With Egypt's crown of triumph.	Il serto trionfale.

Radamès bows before Amneris, who crowns him. [4]

Your dearest wish	Ora a me chiedi
Today shall be granted. Nothing shall be barred or	Quanto più brami. Nulla a te negato
Denied to you . . . By Egypt's	Sarà in tal dì . . . lo giuro
Glorious crown I swear it: the gods are witness.	Per la corona mia, pei sacri Numi.

RADAMÈS

First bring the captive soldiers forth to stand	Concedi in pria che innanzi a te sien tratti
Before your throne . . .	I prigionier . . .

The Ethiopian prisoners enter, escorted by guards. The last of them is Amonasro, dressed as an officer.

RAMFIS, PRIESTS

Worship and glory to all the gods on high	Grazie agli Dei, grazie rendete
Bow down in worship on this most blessed day.	Nel fortunato dì.

AIDA
(rushing towards Amonasro)

Oh Heaven! Captive! My father!	Che veggo! . . . Egli? . . . Mio padre!

ALL
(except Aida)

Her father!	Suo padre!

AMNERIS

And in our power! In poter nostro!

AIDA
(embracing her father)

You! Captive here! Tu! Prigionier!

AMONASRO
(whispering to Aida)

Don't speak my name. Non mi tradir.

THE KING
(to Amonasro)

Come forward . . . T'appressa . . .

Tell me . . . you are . . . Dunque, tu sei?

AMONASRO

Her father. I also fought . . . Suo padre. Anch'io pugnai,

We were defeated . . . all I sought was Vinti noi fummo . . . morte invan cercai.
death.

(indicating his uniform)

As you see, I am wearing the colours Quest'assisa ch'io vesto vi dica
Of my King and my country in battle; Che il mio Re, la mia patria ho difeso;
Fate was hostile to us and our armies . . . Fu la sorte a nostr'armi nemica . . .
All our courage and might were in vain. Tornò vano de' forti l'ardir.
At my feet in the dust of the battle Al mio pie nella polve disteso
Lay our King sadly mangled and Giacque il Re da più colpi trafitto;
bleeding;
If to fight for your country is an evil, Se l'amor della patria è delitto
We are guilty, we're ready to die! Siam rei tutti, siam pronti a morir!

(to the King, in supplication) [23]

Mighty King, you are noble and glorious, Ma tu, Re, tu signore possente,
Show us mercy, tho' you are victorious. A costoro ti volgi clemente;
We today have been struck down by Oggi noi siam percossi dal fato,
fortune,
Ah, tomorrow it may be your turn to Ah! doman voi potria il fato colpir.
die.

AIDA

Mighty King, you are noble and glorious, Ma tu, Re, tu signore possente, *(etc.)*
(etc.)

SLAVE-GIRLS, PRISONERS

We today have been struck down by Sì: dai Numi percossi noi siamo;
fortune;
Here we kneel to implore your compassion; Tua pietà, tua clemenza imploriamo;
May you never be fated to suffer Ah! giammai di soffrir vi sia dato
All the shame we have suffer'd today! Ciò che in oggi n'è dato soffrir!

RAMFIS, PRIESTS [24]

Death, O King, to these savage invaders, Struggi, o Re, queste ciurme feroci,
Close your heart when they try to Chiudi il cor alle perfide voci:
persuade us. —

AIDA, SLAVE-GIRLS, PRISONERS

Forbear! Pietà!

RAMFIS, PRIESTS

They are mark'd bv the gods for destruction. —	Fur dai Numi votati alla morte —

AIDA, SLAVE-GIRLS, PRISONERS

Forbear!	Pietà!

RAMFIS, PRIESTS

Let the will of the gods be obey'd.	Or de' Numi si compia il voler!

AIDA, SLAVE-GIRLS, PRISONERS

Forbear!	Pietà!

AIDA [23]

But you O King, are great in glory, Show us mercy tho' you are victorious . . .	Ma tu, o Re, signore possente, A costoro ti mostra clemente . . .

AMNERIS
(to herself)

How he eyes her, like a doting lover! How they glow when they see one another!	(Quali sguardi sovr'essa ha rivolti! Di qual fiamma balenano i volti!)

AMONASRO

We today tho' have been struck down by fortune But one day it may be your turn to die!	Oggi noi siam percossi dal fato, Voi doman potria il fato colpir.

THE KING

Now that fortune smiles in favour on our city, Let us temper justice with mercy . . .	Or che fausti ne arridon gli eventi A costoro mostriamci clementi . . .

SLAVE-GIRLS, PRISONERS

Here we kneel down to implore pity and kindness, Ah, forbear, forbear!	Tua pietade, tua clemenza imploriamo Ah, pietà! pietà!

POPULACE

Priests of Isis, your anger dismays us. Hear the prayer of the vanquish'd.	Sacerdoti, gli sdegni placate, L'umil prece ascoltate;

RAMFIS, PRIESTS

Destruction! Destruction! Destruction! O King, these invaders all deserve to die!	A morte! a morte! a morte! O Re, struggi queste ciurme!

RADAMÈS
(to himself)

Ah, that grief which the Fates send to tear her Seems in my eyes to make her still fairer; Ev'ry precious lament that she utters Reawakens my heart's tender love. Ev'ry precious lament that she utters Reawakens my longing and love.	Il dolor che in quel volto favella Al mio sguardo la rende più bella; Ogni stilla del pianto adorato Nel mio petto ravviva l'amor.(etc.)

AMNERIS
(to herself)

How he eyes her, he dotes like a lover!	(Quali sguardi sovr'essa ha rivolti!
How they're glowing to see one another!	Di qual fiamma balenano i volti!
I'm abandon'd, I am sad and rejected,	Ed io sola, avvilita, rejetta?
Bitter vengeance is born in my heart!	La vendetta mi rugge nel cor.)

AMONASRO

Here we kneel: show your pity we beg you *(etc.)*	Tua pietà, tua clemenza imploriamo, *(etc.)*

THE KING

Now that fortune has smiled on our city	Or che fausti ne arridon gli eventi,
Let us temper our justice with mercy!	A costoro mostriamci clementi:
Ah, forbear! Mercy rises to Heaven	La pietà sale ai Numi gradita
Reaffirming kingly pow'r.	E rafferma de' prenci il poter.

AIDA

Show pity I beg you . . .	Tua pietà imploro . . .
We have today been struck down by fortune	Oggi noi siam percossi,
But tomorrow it may be your own turn to die.	Doman voi potria il fato colpir.

SLAVE-GIRLS, PRISONERS

Forbear, forbear. Ah, forbear!	Pietà, pietà, ah pietà!
Show your pity we implore.	Tua pietade, tua clemenza invochiamo.

POPULACE

Priests of Isis your anger dismays us.	Sacerdoti, gli sdegni placate,
Hear the prayer of the vanquish'd, we beg you!	L'umil prece de' vinti ascoltate;

RAMFIS, PRIESTS

Let the will of the gods be obey'd!	Si compisca de' Numi il voler!
Death to savage invaders!	Struggi, o Re, queste ciurme feroci,
Let them perish; they are mark'd for destruction.	Fur dai Numi votati alla morte,
Let the powerful will of the gods be obey'd.	Si compisca dei Numi il voler!

AIDA [23]

Mighty King, you are noble and glorious *(etc.)*	Ma tu, o Re, tu signore possente, *(etc.)*

RADAMÈS

Ah, her grief seems to make her still fairer *(etc.)*	Il dolor la rende più bella, *(etc.)*

AMONASRO [23]

Mighty King, you are noble and glorious *(etc.)*	Ma tu, o Re, tu signore possente, *(etc.)*

THE KING

Ah, forbear! Mercy rises *(etc.)*	La pietà sale ai Numi, *(etc.)*

SLAVE-GIRLS, PRISONERS

We today have been struck down by fortune *(etc.)*	Sì, dai Numi percossi noi siamo, *(etc.)*

Death to savage invaders *(etc.)*	Struggi, o Re, queste ciurme feroci, *(etc.)*

POPULACE

King most mighty, you O King, are mighty	Re possente, e tu, o Re possente,
In power, ah, let mercy disarm you today.	Tu forte, a clemenza dischiudi il pensier, *(etc.)*
Ah, show mercy to our vanquish'd foe.	

AMNERIS

I'm abandon'd, I, Amneris *(etc.)*	Ed io sola, avvilita, *(etc.)*

RADAMÈS

O King, by holy Isis	O Re: pei sacri Numi,
And by your crown in its shining splendour,	Per lo splendor della tua corona,
You swore to grant me all I wanted . . .	Compier giurasti il voto mio . . .

THE KING

I swore.	Giurai.

RADAMÈS

Then hear me: for all prisoners here, I beg of you,	Ebbene: a te pei prigionieri Etiopi
Grant them their lives, let them go free.	Vita domando e libertà.

AMNERIS
(to herself)

All of them!	(Per tutti!)

PRIESTS

Death to our country's hated enemies!	Morte ai nemici della patria!

POPULACE

Grant	Grazia
Mercy to the wretched!	Per gl'infelici!

RAMFIS
(to the King, then to Radamès)

Beware O King.	Ascolta, o Re. Tu pure,
And you our	
Glorious hero, yield to the voice of wisdom;	Giovine eroe, saggio consiglio ascolta:
They are hardy, valiant fighters.	Son nemici e prodi sono . . .
They have vengeance in their hearts.	La vendetta hanno nel cor,
If you give them all their freedom,	Fatti audaci dal perdono
They will take up arms again!	Correranno all'armi ancor!

RADAMÈS

With Amonasro, their warrior King, all hope of	Spento Amonasro, il Re guerrier, non resta
Revenge has perish'd.	Speranza ai vinti.

RAMFIS

As pledge of	Almeno,
Peace and security to all, keep	Arra di pace e securtà, fra noi
Aida and hold her father.	Resti col padre Aida.

THE KING

I'll do as you advise me,
But there's a better pledge of peace and safety
For the future. Radamès, your country's
Debt is unbounded. Take in holy marriage
Princess Amneris; rule over Egypt with her at
Your side when I am gone.

Al tuo consiglio io cedo.
Di securtà, di pace un miglior pegno
Or io vo' darvi. Radamès, la patria
Tutto a te deve. D'Amneris la mano
Premio ti sia. Sovra l'Egitto un giorno
Con essa regnerai.

AMNERIS
(to herself)

(Slave, you are nothing!
Now will you dare to steal away my lover?)

(Venga la schiava,
Venga a rapirmi l'amor mio . . . se l'osa!)

THE KING, POPULACE [19, 2, 20]

Glory to Isis, goddess fair,
You who protect and shelter,
The lotus buds and laurel
Entwine over the victor's brow.

Gloria all'Egitto, ad Iside,
Che il sacro suol difende,
S'intrecci il loto al lauro
Sul crin del vincitor.

SLAVE-GIRLS, PRISONERS

Glory to Egypt's clement ways,
You who have loosed our fetters,
You give us back our liberty
And in our native land.

Gloria al clemente Egizio
Che i nostri ceppi ha sciolto,
Che ci ridona ai liberi
Solchi del patrio suol.

RAMFIS, PRIESTS

Offer a hymn to Isis
Defender of our great country!
And pray that the smile of fortune
Will always be kind to our land.

Inni leviamo ad Iside
Che il sacro suol difende!
Preghiam che i fati arridano
Fausti alla patria ognor.

AIDA
(to herself)

Alas what hope is left me now?
For him a glorious future . . .
For me oblivion, the bitter tears
Of my despairing love.

(Qual speme omai più restami?
A lui la gloria, il trono,
A me l'oblio, le lacrime
D'un disperato amor.)

RADAMÈS
(to himself)

The gods have turn'd away from me.
Their thunder falls upon me . . .
Ah no, the throne of Egypt
Rates low by my Aida's heart.

(D'avverso Nume il folgore
Sul capo mio discende . . .
Ah no! d'Egitto il soglio
Non val d'Aida il cor.)

AMNERIS
(to herself)

Ah, how I glow with happiness,
Joy never came so suddenly;
Here in one day I realise
The dream I hold so dear.

(Dall'inatteso giubilo
Inebbriata io sono;
Tutti in un dì si compiono
I sogni del mio cor.)

RAMFIS

We pray that fortune always	Preghiam che i fati arridano
Will smile on our holy land.	Fausti alla patria ognor.

THE KING, POPULACE

Glory! We praise the Gods!	Gloria ad Iside!
Glory! Glory!	Gloria! gloria!

AMONASRO
(aside to Aida)

Take heart, a time of comfort	Fa' cor: della tua patria
Is coming for your country;	I lieti eventi aspetta;
For us the day of vengeance	Per noi della vendetta
Now very soon will dawn.	Già prossimo è l'albor.

RADAMES

The gods have turned away from me!	Qual inatteso folgore!
Their thunder falls upon me!	Sul capo mio discende!
Ah no! the throne of Egypt	Ah no! d'Egitto il trono
Rates low by my Aida's heart!	Non val d'Aida il cor.

AMNERIS

All in a day I realise	(Tutte in un dì si compiono
The sweet dream I hold so dear.	Le gioje del mio cor.
Ah! now I glow with happiness,	Ah! dall'inatteso gaudio
Joy never came so suddenly.	Inebbriata io sono.)

AMONASRO

Take heart, a time of comfort	Fa' cor: la tua patria
Comes soon for your dear country;	I lieti eventi aspetta;
For us the day of vengeance	Per noi della vendetta
Now very soon will dawn.	Già prossimo è l'albor.

THE KING, POPULACE

Glory to Egypt! Glory to Isis,	Gloria all'Egitto! ad Iside
Goddess fair, you who protect,	Che il sacro suol difende!
The lotus buds and laurel	S'intrecci il loto al lauro
Entwine over the victor's brow!	Sul crin del vincitor!

RAMFIS, PRIESTS

Offer a hymn to Isis	Inni leviamo ad Iside
Defender of our great country.	Che il sacro suol difende!
And pray that fortune always smiles	Preghiam che i fati arridano
On our holy country.	Fausti alla patria ognor.

AIDA
(to herself)

For me oblivion, the bitter tears	A me l'oblio, le lacrime
Of my despairing love.	D'un disperato amor.
Ah! alas what hope is left me now?	Ah! qual speme omai più restami?
For him a glorious future . . .	A lui la gloria, il trono . . .
For me oblivion, the bitter tears	A me l'oblio, le lacrime
Of my despairing love!	D'un disperato amor.

SLAVES, PRISONERS

Glory to Egypt's clement ways,	Gloria al clemente Egizio
You who have loosed our fetters.	Che i nostri ceppi ha sciolto,
You now restore us to freedom	Che ci ridona ai liberi
And also to our native land.	Solchi del patrio suol.

Act Three

The banks of the Nile — granite rocks with palm trees. On the summit of the rocks a temple dedicated to Isis half-hidden in foliage. Starry, moonlit night. | Introduction, Prayer-Chorus, Romanza

CHORUS
(in the temple)

Thou art to great Osiris	O tu che sei d'Osiride
Bride and immortal mother,	Madre immortale e sposa,
Goddess who wakest chaste desire	Diva che i casti palpiti
Deep in the human heart . . .	Desti agli umani in cor;

HIGH PRIESTESS

Have pity on us . . .	Soccorri a noi . . .

CHORUS

Grant us thy aid and pity	Soccorri a noi pietosa
Font of almighty love,	Madre d'immenso amor,
Have pity on us.	Soccorri a noi.

Amneris, Ramfis, attendants and guards alight from a boat that has drawn into the riverbank.

RAMFIS
(to Amneris)

Come to the shrine of Isis, and on the night	Vieni d'Iside al Tempio: alla vigilia
Before you are married invoke	Delle tue nozze, invoca
The holy goddess's favour. To holy Isis	Della Diva il favore. Iside legge
Ev'ry human heart is open; all that is hidden	De' mortali nel core: ogni mistero
Deep inside us is known to Isis.	Degli umani a lei noto.

AMNERIS

Yes, and I will pray that Radamès may truly	Sì; io pregherò che Radamès mi doni
Give me his heart, for truly mine to him	Tutto il suo cor, come il mio cor a lui
Is sacred for ever . . .	Sacro è per sempre . . .

RAMFIS

Now enter.	Andiamo.
You will pray till the sunrise: I shall be with you.	Pregherai fino all'alba; io sarò teco.

All enter the temple.

CHORUS

Grant us thy aid and pity,	Soccorri a noi pietosa,
Font of almighty love,	Madre d'immenso amor,
Have pity on us.	Soccorri a noi.

Aida enters cautiously. [1]

AIDA

Soon Radamès will come! What will he tell me?	Qui Radamès verrà! Che vorrà dirmi?

I'm frighten'd. Ah, cruel man,	Io tremo! . . . Ah! se tu vieni
If you're coming to say farewell for ever,	A recarmi, o crudel, l'ultimo addio,
The dark Nile will surely bury me . . .	Del Nilo i cupi vortici
Hide me forever . . .	Mi daran tomba . . .
Peace I may find and perhaps oblivion.	E pace forse e oblìo.
Oh, how I long with all my heart, to see my home!	O patria mia, mai più ti rivedro!

[25]

Oh, skies of blue, oh, soft, caressing breezes,	O cieli azzurri, o dolci aure native,
Land where my childhood serenely passed in joy . . .	Dove sereno il mio mattin brillò,
Oh fertile meadows . . . scented with summer flowers . . .	O verdi colli . . . o profumate rive . . .
Ah, gods above me, when shall I see my home?	O patria mia, mai più ti rivedrò!
Ah, dearest homeland, ah, my home I long for you!	
Oh, fragrant valleys, oh, so blessed haven!	O fresche valli, o questo asil beato,
Once I had hopes of true and faithful love . . .	Che un dì promesso dall'amor mi fu;
Now that my dream of love vanishes for ever . . .	Or che d'amore il sogno è dileguato,
Oh, how I long to be in my native land.	O patria mia, non ti vedrò mai più!
Ah, dearest homeland, (etc.)	O patria mia, (etc.)

Amonasro enters. | Duet

Heav'n! My father!	Ciel! mio padre!

AMONASRO

I come, full of concern	A te grave cagion
For you Aida. Not a look has	M'adduce, Aida. Nulla sfugge al mio
Escaped me. I realise you	Sguardo. D'amor ti struggi
Love Radames . . . he loves you . . . you will meet him,	Per Radames, ei t'ama, qui lo attendi.
The Pharaoh's only daughter is your rival . . .	Dei Faraon la figlia è tua rivale . . .
Curse the Pharaoh! Curse his daughter! They'd destroy us!	Razza infame, abborrita, e a noi fatale!

AIDA

And I am in her power! I, Amonasro's Daughter!	E in suo potere io sto! Io d'Amonasro Figlia!

AMONASRO

You are in her power. No! If you wish it	In poter di lei! No! se lo brami
You can fight with Amneris and defeat her.	La possente rival tu vincerai,
Then homeland and sceptre and love, shall all be yours!	E patria, e trono, e amor, tutto tu avrai.
Once again you will see our lofty forests,	Rivedrai le foreste imbalsamate,
Our fragrant valleys, our temples bright [26] with gold!	Le fresche valli, i nostri templi d'or!

73

Once again I will see our lofty forests,
Our fragrant valleys, our temples bright
with gold!

Rivedrò le foreste imbalsamate!
Le fresche valli, i nostri templi d'òr!

AMONASRO

The happy bride of him you love and
treasure,
Your whole existence only to enjoy . . .

Sposa felice a lui che amasti tanto,

Tripudii immensi ivi potrai gioir . . .

AIDA

A single day of such enchanting
pleasure . . .
To know an hour of such deep joy, and
then to die!

Un giorno solo di sì dolce incanto,

Un'ora di tal gioia, e poi morir!

AMONASRO

Now remember the blasphemous
Egyptian
Profaning our temples, our altars and
our homes . . .
Hanging fetters on innocent young
virgins . . .
Mothers . . . children . . . they all were
put to death.

Pur rammenti che a noi l'Egizio immite,

Le case, i templii, e l'are profano . . .

Trasse in ceppi le vergini rapite . . .

Madri, vecchi, fanciulli ei trucidò.

AIDA

Ah, I remember days of bitter grieving!
Weeping, lamenting, we were in despair.
Great gods, oh hear me, show us now
your mercy,
Grant us a fair season of peace again.

Ah! ben rammento quegl'infausti giorni!
Rammento i lutti che il cor soffrì!
Deh! fate, o Numi che per noi ritorni

L'alba invocata de' sereni dì.

AMONASRO

Remember.
I have an army. Our people now are
waiting
For my orders; ev'rything's prepared . . .
Success is sure . . . One single fact is
missing.
We must know by what path the foe
will march . . .

Rammenta.
Non fia che tardi. In armi ora si desta

Il popol nostro; tutto e pronto gia,
Vittoria avrem. Solo a saper mi resta,

Qual sentier il nemico seguira.

AIDA

Who could ever discover? Ah, who?

Chi scoprirlo potria? chi mai?

AMONASRO

Aida!

Tu stessa!

AIDA

I!

Io!

AMONASRO

Radamès comes here to meet you . . .
He loves you . . .
He commands the Egyptians . . . You
follow?

Radamès so che qui attendi . . . Ei
t'ama . . .
Ei conduci gli Egizii . . . Intendi?

<table>
<tr><td></td><td>Betray him!</td><td>Orrore!</td></tr>
<tr><td>Betray the man I love? No, no, ah, no.</td><td>Che mi consigli tu? No, no, giammai!</td></tr>
</table>

AMONASRO [27]
(with savage fury)

Destroy us, you armies	Su, dunque! sorgete
Of Egypt, destroy us!	Egizie coorti!
Reduce all our cities	Col fuoco struggete
To ashes and dust . . .	Le nostre città . . .
Spread fury and terror,	Spargete il terrore,
Destruction and slaughter,	Le stragi, le morti
For now there is nothing	Al vostro furore
To stand in your way.	Più freno non v'ha.

AIDA

Ah, father, father!	Ah, padre! padre!

AMONASRO
(repulsing her)

	My daughter		Mia figlia
No longer!		Ti chiami! . . .	

AIDA
(thrown to the ground and begging)

Forbear, forbear, forbear!	Pietà! pietà! pietà!

AMONASRO

Rivers of blood drown all our	Flutti di sangue scorrono
Ruined and beaten cities . . .	Sulle città dei vinti.
Mark me, from gloomy caves below	Vedi? dai negri vortici
Shades of the dead are rising . . .	Si levano gli estinti.
All of them point at you and cry:	Ti additan essi e gridano,
'Destroyer of your land!'	'Per te la patria muor!'

AIDA

Forbear! Forbear! Father, forbear!	Pietà! pietà, padre, pietà!

AMONASRO
(sotto voce)

Now I see a skeleton	Una larva orribile
Rising among the shadows . . .	Fra l'ombre a noi s'affaccia.
Horror! It marks your features —	Trema! le scarne braccia —

AIDA
(with no sound)

	Ah!	Ah!

AMONASRO

Pointing a shrivelled arm . . .	Sul capo tuo levò . . .

AIDA

	Father! . . .	Padre! . . .

AMONASRO

Do you not see . . .	Tua madre ell'è . . .

75

No!   No!

AMONASRO

Your mother's hand . . .   Ravvisala . . .

AIDA

Ah!   Ah!

AMONASRO

Raised up to curse you? . . .   Ti maledice . . .

AIDA
(with utmost terror)

Ah no, dear father, spare your child!   Ah! no! ah! no! padre, pietà! pietà!

AMONASRO
(repulsing her)

No more my daughter . . .   Non sei mia figlia!
For you are only a slave of Pharaoh!   Dei Faraoni tu sei la schiava!

AIDA
(with a cry)

Ah! Forgive, forgive, forgive!   Ah! pietà, pietà, pietà!
Father . . . The Egyptians . . have   Padre! a costoro . . . schiava . . . non
    not . . . enslaved me . . .   sono . . .

(dragging herself to her father's feet)

Ah, do not curse me . . . do not revile   Non maledirmi, non imprecarmi;
    me . . .
I am your daughter . . . do not disown   Ancor tua figlia potrai chiamarmi,
    me . . .
I shall be worthy of you and my land.   Della mia patria degna sarò.

AMONASRO [28]

Think how your people all have been   Pensa che un popolo, vinto, straziato,
    subjected
Through you alone they return to life.   Pe te soltanto risorger può . . .

AIDA

Oh dearest country, how much you cost   O patria! o patria quanto mi costi!
    me!

AMONASRO

Have courage, he's coming . . . there I   Coraggio! ei giunge, là tutto udrò . . .
    I shall hide . . .

He hides among the palm trees as Radamès enters. | Duet, Scena — Finale Three

RADAMÈS [29]

At last I see you, sweetest Aida . . .   Pur ti riveggo, mia dolce Aida . . .

AIDA

Don't say that . . . leave me . . . what   T'arresta, vanne, che speri ancor?
    hope is left?

RADAMÈS

A lover's passion has led me here to you.   A te d'appresso l'amor mi guida.

Tomorrow's dawn will bring your marriage vows.
Amneris loves you . . .

Te i riti attendono d'un altro amor.

D'Amneris sposo . . .

RADAMÈS

What's that to me?
My own Aida, I live for you.
The gods above us are witness I love you.

Che parli mai?
Te sola, Aida, te deggio amar.
Gli Dei m'ascoltano, tu mia sarai.

AIDA

With such a falsehood you stain your name.
Hero I loved, I cannot love a liar.

D'uno spergiuro non ti macchiar!

Prode t'amai, non t'amerei spergiuro.

RADAMÈS

But do you doubt my love, dear Aida?

Dell'amor mio dubiti, Aida?

AIDA

Do you
Imagine you'll baffle the charms of Amneris
The will of the King, and the wish of the people,
And all the priests in their fury?

E come
Speri sottrarti d'Amneris ai vezzi,

Del Re al voler, del tuo popolo ai voti,

Dei Sacerdoti all'ira?

RADAMÈS

Listen Aida.
Your people rise again, arming for battle . . .
The troops are gathering . . . soon they will march . . .
And when invaders strike across our borders,
I will be chosen, I shall command.
And in the triumph, when we're victorious,
I'll kneel to Pharaoh, open my heart —
Then you will wear the crown of my glory,
We will live in the bliss of love.

Odimi, Aida.
Nel fiero anelito di nuova guerra

Il suolo Etiope si ridestò . . .

I tuoi già invadono la nostra terra,

Io degli Egizii duce sarò.
Fra il suon, fra i plausi della vittoria,

Al Re mi prostro, gli svelo il cor —
Sarai tu il serto della mia gloria,

Vivrem beati d'eterno amore.

AIDA

Do you not fear Amneris —
The tempest of her rage? Her dreadful vengeance,
Like the lightning from heaven,
Will fall on me and on my father, my people.

Nè d'Amneris paventi
Il vindice furor? la sua vendetta,

Come folgor tremenda,
Cadrà su me, sul padre mio, su tutti.

RADAMÈS

I will defend you.

Io vi difendo.

AIDA

In vain! You could not help me . . .
Yet if you love me, there is always a course

Invan, tu nol potresti . . .

Pur, se tu m'ami, ancor s'apre una via

For us to take . . .	Di scampo a noi . . .

Tell me!	Quale?

AIDA

Escape . . .	Fuggir . . .

RADAMÈS

Escape!	Fuggire!

AIDA
(with impulsive warmth)

We'd leave this white oppressive heat	Fuggiam gli ardori inospiti
And all this barren desert,	Di queste lande ignude;
Turn to another fatherland,	Una novella patria
Where love could blossom truly.	Al nostro amor si schiude.
There where the virgin forests rise, [30]	Là . . . tra foreste vergini,
Perfum'd with fragrant flowers	Di fiori profumate,
In ecstasy of love	In estasi beate
We'll bury all regret.	La terra scorderem.

RADAMÈS

To seek another country	Sovra una terra estrania
And both together fly.	Teco fuggir dovrei!
Abandoning my homeland,	Abbandonar la patria,
Leaving my household gods!	L'are de' nostri Dei!
The soil where first I gathered	Il suol dov'io raccolsi
My laurel leaves of glory,	Di gloria i primi allori,
The place of our first loving,	Il ciel de' nostri amori
How could we both forget?	Come scordar potrem?

AIDA

There where the virgin forests rise *(etc.)*	Là . . . tra foreste vergini, *(etc.)*

RADAMÈS

How to forget the place where we declared our love?	Il ciel de' nostri amori Come scordar potrem?

AIDA

Beneath my sky a freer love	Sotto il mio ciel, più libero
Would flourish more than ever	L'amor ne fia concesso;
And there we'd pray together	Ivi nel tempio istesso
Sharing our gods as well.	Gli stessi Numi avrem.

RADAMÈS

Abandon my dear homeland	Abbandonar la patria
And leave my household gods!	L'are dei nostri Dei!
The place of our first loving,	Il ciel de' nostri amori
How could we both forget?	Come scordar potrem?

AIDA

Ah, come, ah come!	Fuggiam, fuggiam . . .

RADAMÈS

Aida!	Aida!

You don't love me . . . Go!   Tu non m'ami . . . Va!

RADAMÈS

Not love you!   Non t'amo!

AIDA

Go!   Va!

RADAMÈS

There never was a man nor   Mortal giammai nè Dio
Even a god who burned with love as I   Arse d'amor al par del mio possente.
  for you.

AIDA

No! no! Amneris waits   Va, va, t'attende all'ara
To take you . . .   Amneris . . .

RADAMÈS

No! I swear . . .   No! giammai!

AIDA

You swear? You mean it?   Giammai, dicesti?
Then let the axe fall swiftly   Allor piombi la scure
On me and on my father.   Su me, sul padre mio . . .

RADAMÈS
(with impassioned resolution)
Ah no! We'll fly then!   Ah no! fuggiamo!
Hand in hand we'll fly together,   [31]Sì: fuggiam da queste mura,
Find a pathway across the desert;   Al deserto insiem fuggiamo:
Here misfortune rules forever;   Qui sol regna la sventura,
There the heavens smile with love.   Là si schiude un ciel d'amor.
Barren deserts will roll around us,   I deserti interminati
The only marriage bed we lie on,   A noi talamo saranno,
In their courses stars will shine on   Su noi gli astri brilleranno
With a limpid light above.   Di più limpido fulgor.

AIDA

Daily heaven smiles to bless us   Nella terra avventurata
In my father's land of plenty;   De' miei padri, il ciel ne attende;
Sweet and balmy airs caress us,   Ivi l'aura è imbalsamata,
Flowers blossom in ev'ry grove.   Ivi il suolo è aromi e fior.
Fragrant valleys and summer meadows,   Fresche valli e verdi prati
The only marriage bed we lie on,   A noi talamo saranno,
In their courses stars will shine on   Su noi gli astri brilleranno
With a limpid light above.   Di più limpido fulgor.

AIDA AND RADAMÈS

Come away, we'll fly together,   [29]Vieni meco, insiem fuggiamo
Leave behind this land of sorrow!   Questa terra di dolor.
How I love you, how I love you!   Vieni meco, t'amo, t'amo!
Come, and love will be our guide.   A noi duce fia l'amor.

They begin to hurry away, when Aida stops.

AIDA

But tell me, by what path	Ma dimmi; per qual via
Can we avoid the troops of	Eviterem le schiere
Marching soldiers?	Degli armati?

RADAMÈS

We have settled that the road	Il sentier scelto dai nostri
Where my men will attack will be deserted	A piombar sul nemico fia deserto
Up until morning . . .	Fino a domani . . .

AIDA

Say which it is?	E qual sentier?

RADAMÈS

The gorges	Le gole
Of Napata . . .	Di Nàpata.

AMONASRO
(coming forward)

The gorges of Napata!	Di Nàpata le gole!
There I will post my men!	Ivi saranno i miei!

RADAMÈS

But who has heard us?	Oh! chi ci ascolta?

AMONASRO

Aida's father, Ethiopia's King.	D'Aida il padre e degli Etiopi il Re.

RADAMÈS
(with the utmost agitation and surprise)

You! Amonasro! You! The King? Heaven! You cannot . . .	Tu! Amonasro! tu! il Re? Numi! che dissi?

(with a cry)

No . . . it's not true . . . it's not true, This is a nightmare.	No! non è ver! sogno, delirio è questo.

AIDA

Ah no, be calm, and trust in me —	Ah no! ti calma, ascoltami —

AMONASRO

You need the love of Aida . . .	A te l'amor d'Aida . . .

AIDA

My loving hand will lead you.	All'amor mio t'affida.

AMONASRO

Her love will bring you a throne.	Un soglio innalzerà!

RADAMÈS

My name is now dishonour'd!	Io son disonorato!
For you I've played the traitor and betrayed my fatherland!	Per te tradii la patria! tradii la patria!

AIDA

Ah, trust me!	Ti calma!

80

AMONASRO

No, no! No guilt can fall on you;
It was the will of fate, it had to
  happen . . .

No: tu non sei colpevole:
Era voler del fato . . .

RADAMÈS

My name is now dishonour'd!

Io son disonorato!

AIDA

Ah no!

Ah no!

AMONASRO

No!

No!

RADAMÈS

For you I played the traitor!
For you I sold my fatherland!

Per te tradii la patria!
Per te tradii la patria!

AMONASRO

No. No guilt can fall on you.

No: tu non sei colpevole.

AIDA

Ah, trust me . . .

Ti calma . . .

AMONASRO

There where the Nile is glittering,
Soldiers of mine are waiting.
Ev'ry desire that your heart has longed
  for
Will soon be crowned in love.
Come then, quickly, quickly.

Vien: oltre il Nil ne attendono
I prodi a noi devoti,
Là del tuo cor i voti

Coronerà l'amor.
Vieni, vieni, vieni.

(dragging Radamès)

AMNERIS
(coming out of the temple, with Ramfis)

We're betrayed!

Traditor!

AIDA

My rival here!

La mia rival!

AMONASRO
(rushing at Amneris with a dagger)

Would you try to spoil my triumph?
Die then!

L'opra mia a strugger vieni!
Muori!

RADAMÈS
(rushing between them)

Don't strike her, you madman!

Arresta, insano!

AMONASRO

Oh, fury!

O rabbia!

RAMFIS

Guards there, come here!

Guardie, olà!

RADAMÈS
(to Aida and Amonasro)

Quickly! Go quickly!

Presto! fuggite!

81

AMONASRO
(dragging Aida)

Quickly my daughter!   Vieni, o figlia!

RAMFIS
(to the guards, who pursue Aida and Amonasro, who have escaped)

Follow closely!   L'inseguite!

RADAMÈS
(to Ramfis)

Priest of Isis, I yield my sword.   Sacerdote, io resto a te.

The last moments of 'Aida' Act Three, at Her Majesty's Theatre, London (1879), with Marie Roze (Aida), Trebelli (Amneris), Frapolli (Radamès), Pantaleoni (Amonasro) and Pinto (Ramfis) (BBC Hulton Picture Library)

Act Four

A hall in the King's palace. On the left a large portal leading to the subterranean hall of justice. A passage on the right leading to the prison of Radamès. | *Scena and Duet*

Amneris mournfully crouched before the portal

AMNERIS [5]

The detestable slave escapes my vengeance . . .	L'abborrita rivale a me sfuggia . . .
And from the priests now Radamès is waiting	Dai sacerdoti Radamès attende
The punishment of traitors. He is no	Dei traditor la pena . . . Traditor
Traitor, I swear . . . Yet he revealed the mighty	Egli non è . . . Pur rivelò di guerra
Secret of battle . . . Flight was the course he'd chosen . . .	L'alto segreto. Egli fuggir volea,
And with Aida. They're a pair of traitors!	Con lei fuggire! Traditori tutti!
Destroy them! Destroy them!	A morte! A morte!
Oh! Gods forgive me! I love him,	Oh! che mai parlo? io l'amo,
I love him . . . This insane, despairing [4]	Io l'amò sempre. Disperato, insano
Love for him is driving me to madness.	È quest'amor che la mia vita strugge.
Ah! if he only could love me!	Oh! s'ei potesse amarmi!
I long to save him . . . But can I?	Vorrei salvarlo. E come?
I'll see him! Soldiers: Radamès may enter.	Si tenti! Guardie: Radamès qui venga.

Radamès is brought in by the guards. [32]

Soon all the priests will gather here,	Già i sacerdoti adunansi,
Judgement will soon be spoken;	Arbitri del tuo fato;
You are accused of treachery;	Pur dell'accusa orribile
Your silence must be broken;	Scolparti ancor t'è dato;
Defend yourself I beg you;	Ti scolpa, e la tua grazia
I will appeal to Pharaoh	Io pregherò dal trono,
And beg his kingly favour	E nunzia di perdono,
And beg that he will grant	E nunzia di perdono,
Forgiveness and spare your life.	Di vita, a te sarò.

RADAMÈS

The judges will never hear from me	Di mie discolpe i giudici
Any defence or reason;	Mai non udran l'accento;
I call the gods to witness here	Dinanzi ai Numi, agl'uomini,
I never plotted treason.	Nè vil, nè reo mi sento.
In innocence I uttered	Profferse il labbro incauto
The words that have offended,	Fatal segreto, è vero,
But all that I intended	Ma puro il mio pensiero
Was to be true, I swear.	E l'onor mio restò.

AMNERIS

Then save your life, defend yourself.	Salvati dunque e scolpati.

RADAMÈS

No!	No!

You will die . . .   Tu morrai . . .

RADAMÈS

         My life is   La vita
Hateful! Ev'ry pleasure   Abborro; d'ogni gaudio
Is turned to bitter ashes,   La fonte inaridita,
And hope is gone for ever.   Svanita ogni speranza,
I pray that I may die.   Sol bramo di morir.

AMNERIS [33]

No never! Ah! you must live, ah, yes   Morire! ah! tu dei vivere!
You must live because I love you.   Sì, all'amor mio vivrai;
I feel I know the pains of death   Per te le angoscie orribili
And now I want to save you: Di morte io già provai;
I love . . . I suffer torture . . .   T'amai, soffersi tanto,
The nights I spend in weeping . . .   Vegliai le notti in pianto,
My country, my sceptre, my throne and   E patria, e trono, e vita
  my life,
All I'd surrender, all the world I'd   Tutto darei per te.
  surrender for you.

RADAMÈS [33]

A traitor to my country . . .   Per essa anch'io la patria
I am dishonour'd and all for her . . .   E l'onor mio tradia . . .

AMNERIS

No more of her . . .   Di lei non più!

RADAMÈS

       Dishonour   L'infamia
Awaits me, you want me living?   M'attende, e vuoi ch'io viva?
Misery overwhelms me,   Misero appien mi festi,
You've taken Aida from me . . .   Aida a me togliesti,
You may have killed her . . . before   Spenta l'hai forse, e in dono
Offering life to me.   Offri la vita a me?

AMNERIS

Do you think I've murdered her!   Io, di sua morte origine!
No, she is living . . .   No! vive Aida . . .

RADAMÈS

       Living!   Vive!

AMNERIS

Egypt had tasted victory . . .   Nei disperati aneliti
The foe was fleeing blindly . . .   Dell'orde fuggitive
Down went her father . . .   Sol cadde il padre . . .

RADAMÈS

      And she?   Ed ella?

AMNERIS

Vanish'd and no-one here has   Sparve nè piu novella
Seen her . . .   S'ebbe . . .

RADAMÈS

     The gods will lead her to   Gli Dei l'adducano
Safety among her people,   Salva alle patrie mura,

She'll never know the torments	E ignori la sventura
Of one who dies for her!	Di chi per lei morrà!

But if I save you, swear to me	Ma, s'io ti salvo, giurami
You won't see her again . . .	Che più non la vedrai . . .

RADAMÈS

I cannot!	Nol posso!

AMNERIS

You must renounce her	A lei rinunzia
For ever . . . life will be yours!	Per sempre, e tu vivrai!

RADAMÈS

I cannot!	Nol posso!

AMNERIS

Once more I ask you;	Anco una volta:
Renounce Aida . . .	A lei rinuncia . . .

RADAMÈS

It's useless . . .	È vano.

AMNERIS

You cannot want to perish?	Morir vuoi dunque, insano?

RADAMÈS

I pray that death come soon.	Pronto a morir son già.

AMNERIS

Who will save you, wretched madman,	Chi ti salva, sciagurato,
Who will save you from destruction?	Dalla sorte che t'aspetta?
Since you spurn the love I offer,	In furore hai tu cangiato
All my joy is turned to care.	Un amor ch'egual non ha.
Gods in heaven grant me vengeance;	De' miei pianti la vendetta
See my tears of black despair.	Or dal ciel si compirà.

RADAMÈS

Death I greet you, welcome I give you,	È la morte un ben supremo
Since I die for her I cherish;	Se per lei morir m'è dato;

AMNERIS

Ah, who will save you?	Ah! chi ti salva?

RADAMÈS

Full of joy, knowing I perish,	Nel subir l'estremo fato
Full of immense accord with her.	Gaudii immensi il cor avrà;

AMNERIS

Gods in heaven, grant me vengeance,	De' miei pianti la vendetta
See, oh, see my tears of black despair.	Or dal ciel si compirà.

RADAMÈS

Full of rejoicing I die for her.	Gaudii immensi il cor avrà;
Human anger cannot touch me,	L'ira umana più non temo,
Show me pity if you dare.	Temo sol la tua pietà.

Amneris falls despairingly on a chair, Radamès leaves surrounded by guards. / Scene of the Judgement

AMNERIS
(alone, in the utmost despair)

Alas! I feel I'm dying . . . Ah, who will save him?	Ohimè! morir mi sento! Oh! chi lo salva?
He is now in their power,	E in poter di costoro

(choked with tears)

I'm guilty . . . he is lost! . . . Oh how I curse the	Io stessa lo gettai! Ora, a te impreco
Jealousy that drove me! His death is certain;	Atroce gelosia, che la sua morte
For me a life of endless grief and mourning!	E il lutto eterno del mio cor segnasti!

The Priests process into the subterranean hall. [2]

Oh, how I fear these stern,	Ecco i fatali,
Cruel judges, the lords of destruction . . .	Gl'inesorati ministri di morte . . .
Ah, I'll not look upon these pallid phantoms!	Oh! ch'io non vegga quelle bianche larve!

(she covers her face with her hands)

He is now in their power . . .	E in poter di costoro
And I have sealed his fate!	Io stessa lo gettai!
I'm guilty! He is lost!	Io stessa lo gettai!

RAMFIS, PRIESTS
(from the hall)

Spirit of Isis on us all descending!	Spirto del Nume sovra noi discendi!
Lighten our darkness with your flame eternal;	Ne avviva al raggio dell'eterna luce;
Now thro' our lips express thy justice unending!	Pel labbro nostro tua giustizia apprendi.

AMNERIS

Ye gods above, I beg, I kneel before you;	Numi, pietà del mio straziato core.
For he is innocent and you must save,	Egli è innocente, lo salvate, o Numi!
You must save him or I shall die of sorrow.	Disperato, tremendo è il mio dolore!

Radamès and the guards cross the stage, and enter the hall.

RAMFIS, PRIESTS

Spirit of Isis —	Spirto del Nume —

AMNERIS
(seeing Radamès, with a cry)

Ah! who will save him?	Oh! chi lo salva?

RAMFIS, PRIESTS

— on us all descending!	— sovra noi discendi!

AMNERIS

Ah, who will save him? I feel I will die!	Oh, chi lo salva? mi sento morir!
Alas! Alas! I feel I will die!	Ohimè! ohimè! mi sento morir!

RAMFIS
(in the crypt)

Radamès! Radamès! Radamès!	Radamès! Radamès! Radamès!

86

You did betray   Tu rivelasti
Your country's highest secrets to   Della patria i segreti allo straniero . . .
    Amonasro . . .
Defend yourself!   Discolpati!

Defend yourself!   Discolpati!

            He is silent . . .   Egli tace . . .

            He must die!   Traditor!

Ah, have pity, gods, you must save him,   Ah, pietà! egli è innocente! Numi,
    oh hear my pray'r!   pietà!

Radamès! Radamès! Radamès! You did   Radames! Radamès! Radamès! tu
    desert   disertasti
Egypt's army the day before the start of   Dal campo il dì che precedea la
    battle . . .   pugna . . .
Defend yourself!   Discolpati!

Defend yourself!   Discolpati!

            He is silent . . .   Egli tace . . .

            He must die!   Traditor!

Ah, have pity, gods, you must save him,   Ah, pieta! ah, lo salvate, Numi, pietà!
    ah, hear my pray'r!

Radamès! Radamès! Radamès! You   Radamès! Radamès! Radamès! tua fe
    broke your oath   violasti
And were false to your country, your   Alla patria spergiuro, al Re, all'onor.
    King and your word!
Defend yourself!   Discolpati!

Defend yourself!   Discolpati!

            He is silent . . .   Egli tace . . .

            He must die!   Traditor!

Ah, have pity, gods, you must save him,   Ah, pieta! ah, lo salvate, Numi, pieta!
    ah, hear my pray'r!

Radamès, our decision is taken;   Radamès, è deciso il tuo fato:

You will suffer the death of a traitor;	Degli infami la morte tu avrai;
By the shrine of the god you've forsaken,	Sotto l'ara del Nume sdegnato,
You'll be buried alive in a tomb.	A te vivo fia schiuso l'avel.

AMNERIS

To be buried alive? Cruel monsters!	A lui vivo . . . la tomba . . . oh, gl'infami!
You will always be thirsty for blood . . .	Nè di sangue son paghi giammai;
And you say you are servants of God!	E si chiaman ministri del ciel!

RAMFIS, PRIESTS
(returning from the crypt) [2]

| He must die! He must die! He must die! | Traditor! traditor! traditor! |

AMNERIS

Priests of Isis: you're guilty of murder!	Sacerdoti: compiste un delitto!
Pitiless tigers, you reek of destruction.	Tigri infami di sangue assetate,
All the earth and the gods condemn your verdict . . .	Voi la terra ed i Numi oltraggiate . . .
Ah, you punish an innocent man.	Voi punite chi colpe non ha!

RAMFIS, PRIESTS

| Sentence of death! Sentence of death! Of death! | E traditor! e traditor! morra. |

AMNERIS
(to Ramfis)

Priest of Isis, the man you are killing	Sacerdote: quest'uomo che uccidi,
Might have ruled as my heart's dear beloved . . .	Tu lo sai, da me un giorno fu amato,
May the curse of a woman broken-hearted,	L'anatema d'un core straziato
Fall on your senses, avenging his blood!	Col suo sangue su te ricadrà!

RAMFIS, PRIESTS

| Sentence of death! Sentence of death! Of death! | E traditor! e traditor! morra. |

AMNERIS

| All the earth and the gods condemn your verdict . . . | Voi la terra ed i Numi oltraggiate . . . |

RAMFIS, PRIESTS

| Of death! | Morrà! |

AMNERIS

Ah, you punish an innocent man.	Voi punite chi colpe non ha!
Ah no, oh no, not he.	Ah, no, ah no, non è,
He must not die, I beg, I implore!	Non e traditor . . . pieta!

RAMFIS, PRIESTS

| He has to die! | E traditor! morra! morrà! |
| Traitor die, traitor die, traitor die! | Traditor! traditor! traditor! |

The priests leave.

AMNERIS

| Evil priesthood, may you all be accurs'd! | Empia razza! anatema su voi! |
| May the vengeance of heaven descend | La vendetta del ciel scenderà! |

on you
May you all be accurs'd!   Anatema su voi!

Scene two. *The stage is divided into two levels. The upper floor represents the interior of the Temple of Vulcan resplendent with gold and glittering light. The lower floor is a crypt. Long arcades vanishing in the gloom. Colossal statues of Osiris with crossed hands support the pillars of the vault. Radamès is discovered in the crypt on the steps which lead down into the vault. Above, two priests in the act of letting down the stone which closes the subterranean apartment. | Scena and Duet. Last Finale*

RADAMÈS

The fatal stone is now in place above me . . .	La fatal pietra sovra me si chiuse . . .
This is my tomb forever. I'll never see The daylight again . . . Never behold Aida . . .	Ecco la tomba mia. Del di la luce Piu non vedro . . . Non rivedro piu Aida . . .
Aida, where are you now? May you at least be Carefree and happy. Pray that you never learn My horrible fate! I heard a sound! A phantom . . .	Aida, ove sei tu? Possa tu almeno Viver felice e la mia sorte orrenda Sempre ignorar! Qual gemito! Una larva . . .
It is a ghost . . . No! It's a human figure . . .	Una vision . . . No! forma umana è questa . . .
Heav'n! Aida!	Ciel! . . . Aida!

AIDA

Beside you . . .   Son io . . .

RADAMÈS
(with utmost despair)

              You . . . in this   Tu, in questa
dark prison!   tomba!

AIDA
(sadly)

My heart foretold this horrifying sentence	Presago il core della tua condanna,
I saw them raise the cover to confine you!	In questa tomba che per te s'apriva
I crept inside to find you . . .	Io penetrai furtiva . . .
And here, away from ev'ry human presence,	E qui lontana da ogni umano sguardo
Held in your arms, I would like to die!	Nelle tue braccia desiai morire.

RADAMÈS [34]

To die! so pure and lovely!	Morir! sì pura e bella!
To die . . . because you love me . . .	Morir per me d'amore . . .
Delicate, precious flower, so delicate a flower	Degli anni tuoi nel fiore
To fade for ever!	Fuggir la vita!
The gods created you for love and pleasure,	T'avea il cielo per l'amor creata,
And now I kill my dearest love and treasure!	Ed io t'uccido per averti amata!
No, do not die!	No, non morrai!
You must not die, you are too lovely!	Troppo t'amai! troppo sei bella!

AIDA [35]
(in a delirium)

Hail to the messenger of death:	Vedi? di morte l'angelo
See how his golden wings shine . . .	Radiante a noi s'appressa;
He comes to tell us of our joy	Ne adduce a eterni gaudii
And carry us above . . .	Sovra i suoi vanni d'ór.
I see the gates of paradise	Gia veggo il ciel dischiudersi,
And there the smile of the gods	Ivi ogni affanno cessa,
divine . . .	
We two will live in ecstacy,	Ivi comincia l'estasi
Eternally in love.	D'un immortale amor.

PRIESTESSES
(from the temple above)

Almighty Phtha the breathing	Immenso Ftha, del mondo
Spirit of life in us all.	Spirito animator
We here implore thee.	Noi t'invochiam.

PRIESTS

Ah! We here implore thee.	Ah! noi t'invochiamo.

AIDA

Solemn chanting!	Triste canto!

RADAMÈS

Yes, the rites of	Il tripudio
The priests of Isis . . .	Dei Sacerdoti . . .

AIDA

Our hymn of death is ascending.	Il nostro inno di morte.

RADAMÈS
(trying to displace the stone closing the vault)

Gods, give my arms the power!	Ne le mie forti braccia
Surely my strength can move this dark,	Smuovere ti potranno, o fatal pietra!
fatal cover!	

AIDA

Alas! All things are over	Invan! tutto e finito
Now for us here on earth.	Sulla terra per noi.

RADAMÈS

All over, all over!	E vero! e vero!

AIDA [36]

Farewell oh life, farewell oh valley of	O terra addio, addio valle di pianti . . .
sorrow . . .	
Our dream of joy has faded far away . . .	Sogno di gaudio che in dolor svanì
But now the beauty of heav'n is open	A noi si schiude il ciel e l'alme erranti
wide and now our souls fly	
Up to the light of our eternal day.	Volano al raggio dell' eterno dì.

RADAMÈS

Farewell oh life, farewell oh valley (etc.)	O terra addio, addio valle di pianti, (etc.)

AIDA

Oh earth I leave you . . . (etc.)	O terra addio (etc.)

Almighty Phtha we here implore!   Immenso Fthà, noi t'invochiam!

AIDA, RADAMES

Ah! the beauty of heav'n!   Ah! — si schiude il ciel.
Farewell oh life, farewell oh valley of   O terra addio, addio valle di pianti. *(etc.)*
  sorrow. *(etc.)*

AMNERIS
(dressed in mourning, prostrates herself on the stone which seals the vault)

Peace, I implore you . . . beloved hero   Pace t'imploro . . . salma adorata
May Isis hear you and pardon you!   Isi placata ti schiuda il ciel!

CHORUS

We here implore almighty Phtha!   Noi t'invochiam, immenso Fthà!

AIDA, RADAMES
(as she dies)

The light . . . eternal day!   Il ciel . . . si schiude il ciel!

AMNERIS

Peace I implore you. Peace, I   Pace t'imploro. Pace, pace,
  implore you. Peace.   pace.

CHORUS

Almighty Phtha!   Immenso Fthà!

THE END

'Aida' at Her Majesty's Theatre, London (1879), with the American Clara Louise
Kellogg in the title role, Trebelli (Amneris) and Campanini (Radamès)

Bibliography

A selective list of books in English for further reading.

The most comprehensive edition of the documents relating to *Aida* is *Verdi's Aida: The History of an Opera in Letters and Documents*, collected and translated by Hans Busch (University of Minnesota Press, Minneapolis, 1978). Besides all the relevant correspondence, this fascinating volume contains biographies of all the characters who took part in the creation of the work.

An appreciation of the opera is contained in Vincent Godefroy's *The Dramatic Genius of Verdi*, Vol 1 (Gollancz, 1975), and another will be included in the third and final volume of Julian Budden's *The Operas of Verdi* (Vols I & II, Cassell, 1973, 1978).

The Letters of Giuseppe Verdi, translated and edited by Charles Osborne (Gollancz, 1971) make a fascinating introduction to Verdi's life, with fresh insights into his character, methods of composition and the times in which he lived. William Weaver's *Verdi: A Documentary Study* (Thames & Hudson, 1977), supplements a selection of the letters with other documents, including press reviews of the Cairo premiere of *Aida* and some beautiful illustrations.

Two general biographies are of interest: *Verdi: His Life and Works* by Francis Toye (Heinemann, 1931) and *The Man Verdi* by Frank Walker (Dent, 1962). Joseph Wechsberg's *Verdi* (Weidenfeld & Nicholson, 1974) and Charles Osborne's *The Operas of Verdi* (Macmillan, 1978) contain some fascinating illustrations, with lively texts.

The full score is published by Ricordi & Co.

Discography

In order of UK release. All performances are in stereo unless asterisked* and in Italian.

Complete recordings Conductor Company/Orchestra	Erede Santa Cecilia	Serafin La Scala, Milan	Toscanini NBC SO & Ch. (rec. 1949)	Karajan Vienna GM & PO Rome Opera	Solti Rome Opera	Serafin Rome Opera (rec. 1946)
Aida	R. Tebaldi	M. Callas	H. Nelli	R. Tebaldi	L. Price	M. Caniglia
Amneris	E. Stignani	F. Barbieri	E. Gustavson	G. Simionato	R. Gorr	E. Stignani
Radamès	M. del Monaco	R. Tucker	R. Tucker	C. Bergonzi	J. Vickers	B. Gigli
Amonasro	A. Protti	T. Gobbi	G. Valdengo	C. MacNeil	R. Merrill	G. Bechi
King of Egypt	F. Corena	N. Zaccaria	D. Harbour	F. Corena	P. Clabassi	I. Tajo
Ramphis	D. Caselli	G. Modesti	N. Scott	A. van Mill	G. Tozzi	T. Pasero
High priestess	—	E. Galassi	T. Stich-Randall	E. Ratti	M. Sighele	M. Huder
Messenger	P. di Palma	F. Ricciardi	V. Assandri	P. di Palma	F. Ricciardi	A. Zagonara
Disc UK Number	D47D3	SLS5108	AT302 *	SXL2167 - 9	SET427 - 9	SH 153 - 5 *
Tape UK Number		TC - SLS5108		K2A20	K64K32	
Excerpts (Disc)				SXL 2242		
Excerpts (Tape)				KSXC 2242		
Disc US Number	RS 63002 *	3525CL *	VIC 56113	LON 1313	LON 1393	
Tape US Number				5 - 1313	5 - 1393	
Excerpts (Disc)				LON 25206		
Excerpts (Tape)				5 - 25206		

Excerpts only

Conductor	Muti	Leinsdorf	Pritchard
Company/Orchestra	Covent Garden	Alldis Choir/LSO	Covent Garden
Aida	M. Caballé	L. Price	B. Nilsson
Amneris	F. Cossotto	G. Bumbry	G. Hoffmann
Radamès	P. Domingo	P. Domingo	Ottolini
Amonasro	P. Cappuccilli	S. Milnes	L. Quilico
King of Egypt	L. Roni	H. Sotin	—
Ramphis	N. Ghiaurov	—	—
High priestess	E. Casas	J. Mathis	—
Messenger	N. Martinucci	B. Brewer	—
Disc UK Number	SLS 977	SER 5609-11	SXL 6068
Tape UK Number	TC-SLS 9771 - 3	RK40005	
Excerpts (Disc)	ASD 3292		
Excerpts (Tape)	TC-ASD 3292		
Disc US Number	SX 3815	LSC 6198	LON OS 25798
Tape US Number	4X35 - 3815	ARK3 - 2544	
Excerpts (Disc)	S - 37228 (Q0		LSC - 3275
Excerpts (Tape)			RK - 1237

Excerpts

	Artist	UK numbers only Disc Number	Tape
Prelude	LSO/Abbado	RL31378	
	Hungarian State Opera/		
	Erdelyi	SHLX90051	
	Berlin PO/Karajan	2707 090	
	Berlin PO/Karajan	2531 145	3301 145
Se quel guerrier/Celeste Aida	C. Bergonzi	6580 150	7317 160
	E. Caruso	RL11749	RK11749
Celeste Aida	C. Bergonzi	SPA535	KCSP535
	P. Domingo	SXL 6451	
	C. Bergonzi	SDD 391	
	L. Pavarotti	SXL 6649	KSXC 6649
Ritorna Vincitor	L. Welitsch	SH 289 ★	
	L. Price	DPS 2001	
	R. Tebaldi	SET 439 - 40	
	F. Weathers	AG 6 41947	
	S. Sass	SXL 6841	KSXC 6841
	M. Chiara	SXL 6605	
	M. Callas	P48	C48
Dances of the Priestesses/	Berlin PO/Karajan	2530 200	
Moorish Slaves	Berlin PO/Karajan	3300 206	3850 068
Gloria all' Egitto	La Scala/Abbado	2530 549	3300 495
	Santa Cecilia/Franci	SXL 6139	
	Covent Garden/Gardelli	TWO 390	
O patria mia	L. Price	DPS 2001	
	M. Chiara	SXL 6548	KSXC 6548
	M. Callas	SLS 5104	TC-SLS 510
Pur ti riveggo	J. Hammond, C. Craig	ESD 7033	TC-ESD 70
L'abborrita rivale/			
Gia i sacerdoti	R. Tebaldi, F. Corelli	SXL 6585	
L'abborrita rivale	E. Komlossy	SLPX 11329	
La fatale pietra (& duet)	J. Sutherland, L. Pavarotti	SXL 6828	KSXC 682